This Is the Day That the Lord Has Made

This Is the Day That the Lord Has Made

The Liturgical Year in Orthodoxy

BY

Nicholas Denysenko

CASCADE *Books* · Eugene, Oregon

THIS IS THE DAY THAT THE LORD HAS MADE
The Liturgical Year in Orthodoxy

Cascade Books
An Imprint of Wipf and Stock Publishers
199 W. 8th Ave., Suite 3
Eugene, OR 97401

www.wipfandstock.com

PAPERBACK ISBN: 978-1-6667-1775-4
HARDCOVER ISBN: 978-1-6667-1776-1
EBOOK ISBN: 978-1-6667-1777-8

Cataloguing-in-Publication data:

Names: Denysenko, Nicholas, author.

Title: This is the day that the lord has made : the liturgical year in orthodoxy / by Nicholas Denysenko.

Description: Eugene, OR: Cascade Books, 2023 | Includes bibliographical references.

Identifiers: ISBN 978-1-6667-1775-4 (paperback) | ISBN 978-1-6667-1776-1 (hardcover) | ISBN 978-1-6667-1777-8 (ebook)

Subjects: LCSH: Orthodox Eastern Church–Liturgy–History | Orthodox Eastern Church–Calendars | Orthodox Eastern Church–Liturgy–Texts–History and criticism.

Classification: BX375 .D20 2023 (print) | BX375 .D20 (ebook)

05/12/23

To Tal Howard, Susan Holman, and Ron Rittgers—
beloved colleagues.

Contents

List of Illustrations | viii

Preface | ix

Acknowledgments | xiii

Chapter 1: Introducing the Liturgical Year | 1

Chapter 2: The Movable Cycle | 11

Chapter 3: The Fixed Cycle | 55

Chapter 4: Everything Else | 96

Chapter 5: Problems, Opportunities, Time | 126

Conclusion | 147

Bibliography | 157

List of Illustrations

Fig. 2.1   Paschal Vigil, Holy Trinity Orthodox Church,
            St. Paul, Minnesota | 40

Fig. 2.2   Paschal Matins, Mala Sophia Orthodox Church,
            Kyiv, Ukraine. Photo by Fr. John Sydor.
            Used with permission. | 42

Fig. 3.1   Blessing of Waters on Theophany, St. Nicholas Orthodox
            Church, San Anselmo, California. Photo by Jennifer Lord.
            Used with permission. | 67

Fig. 3.2   Blessing of Candles, Meeting Feast, Mala Sophia
            Orthodox Church, Kyiv, Ukraine. Photo by Fr. John Sydor.
            Used with permission. | 73

Fig. 3.3   Dormition Feast icon, Spaso-Preobrazhenskiy Orthodox
            parish, Kyiv, Ukraine. Photo used with permission. | 84

Fig. 3.4   Annunciation Feast icon, Protection of the Virgin Mary
            Orthodox parish, Merrillville, Indiana. Photo used with
            permission. | 86

Fig. 4.1   Procession on Feast of the Baptism of Rus', St. Vladimir
            Memorial Church, Jackson, New Jersey. Photo used with
            permission. | 114

Preface

THE ORDINARY ORTHODOX CHRISTIAN knows the meaning of "feast" through experience. A true feast means setting aside some extra time in honor of a meaningful event of the community's history. On a national level, in the US Thanksgiving continues to be a day of family gatherings for food and fellowship. The advancements of modernity have not slowed the observance of this day. In every community from Los Angeles to the rural townships of West Virginia, streets, parking lots, and driveways fill with cars that make the trek to gather families for dinner. Similarly, people take a day off and prepare barbecues, games, water sports, and fireworks for the Fourth of July. On a local level, communities continue to cherish festivals and parades in honor of important people and events. On the level of the family, the most nuclear cell of human community, people gather for dinner and fellowship to commemorate birthdays and anniversaries. In spite of the festive mood of any holiday event, they are thoroughly human; feuds, arguments, and bad behavior are part of the package. Both the pleasant and the forgettable are a necessary part of any community feast.

The church is a community of which the parish is the nuclear cell. Like nations, towns, and families, parish communities also gather for feasts. They come together to observe major holidays like Pascha and Christmas. The energy devoted to preparatory activities and the execution of ministries cannot be understated. Parish councils create budgets to buy and prepare food. Choirs schedule extra rehearsals to learn special music. The clergy gather altar servers to rehearse complex actions reserved for special occasions. Volunteers wash linens, sweep and scrub floors, purchase and place floral arrangements, arrange seating, and prepare the technology for recording and livestreaming.

For many parishes, the patronal or temple feast is a big deal. It certainly was in my childhood. The choir would prepare its best music. The pastor always invited the bishop to preside, and when he was not available, the dean would come, along with deanery clergy. In my experience, the best deacons would serve and adorn the church with their powerful operatic voices. Some parishes had formal banquets following the feast, complete with a head table for the bishop and clergy; wine and savory food; speeches; and dance, poetry, and singing performances. More often than not, the banquets were long, and there were too many speeches.

Some feasts spill into family homes. Families gather after Paschal services for dinner, which, among some Slavic communities, involves a festive breakfast that includes savory lamb, cheese, pork and sausage, pizza, and burgers. Throughout the Orthodox world, the meal and music is its own kind of liturgy and blends seamlessly with official liturgy. Dining rooms, decks, and parish basements and halls fill with laughing, storytelling, and serious conversation, along with moments of loneliness and alienation, and occasional episodes of "overdoing" it.

Every year, parishes and their people gather over and over again for these occasions, falling into a rhythm of preparation and performance. Many people—both clergy and faithful—come away asking the same questions. What does it all mean? What is the meaning of this experience of gathering for intense prayer, nonstop singing, complex rituals, and alternating episodes of fasting and feasting? More often than not, pastors are eager to provide answers to these questions. From the apostolic age until today, many have written sermons explaining the meaning of feasts and exhorting the people to observe them. The number and complexity of feasts has increased through history, each associated with scriptural lessons, hymns, and special rites governed by the church.

Sometimes, the different components of feasts are so intense that they become difficult for pastors and musicians to navigate. The services of Holy Week, for example, are both a sprint and a marathon, requiring endless amounts of energy that often leave participants exhausted. Many of the assigned readings repeat themselves. Along with the many other elements of the holiday, pastors are also expected to bless special baskets before the midnight paschal services. Sometimes, holidays overlap. The Annunciation occasionally falls during Holy Week and, once in a great while, on Pascha itself! In addition, the size of services can be hard to estimate. On Christmas, attendance can be uneven, especially in countries with large Catholic and

Protestant communities. This brief description of the reality of the Orthodox liturgical year barely scratches the surface. It can be quite complex, and people ask all kinds of questions about appropriate times for confession, when and where they can obtain holy water, and when they need to fast.

Pastors are eager to answer questions like these, and they turn to sources of information for assistance. Learning the ins and outs of the liturgical year is a difficult task. Many priests, deacons, and musicians master the art, but some struggle to retain it all. I was born and raised in the Orthodox Church, was a choir director for over ten years, and was ordained to the diaconate in 2003, and I still fumble the rubrics on occasion.

The matter of passing on the meaning of a tradition is crucial. Many new people have discovered the Orthodox Church. Converts come from all backgrounds. Some are elected to serve the church as deacons and priests, and others simply want to become familiar with the traditions. Parish priests are the ones usually responsible for passing on the central meaning of tradition to new clergy and faithful.

The impetus for this book came from a parish priest, someone who attended seminary with me and was in the process of introducing the liturgical year to a candidate for diaconal ordination. He would write me and ask questions about the liturgical year, and I found myself responding with articles written by experts, but there was no single book that covered the entire church year, or even most of it. To be fair, there are books that discuss the liturgical year in the Orthodox Church. The venerable Lev Gillet wrote a marvelous devotional work on the liturgical year, a gem that includes commentary on several Sundays after Pentecost. Recently, an English translation of Archbishop Job Getcha's introduction to the typikon was released. Archbishop Job's book is an essential tool for pastors and musicians to understand the history of the church year, especially Orthodoxy's unique mechanism of governing the convergence of feasts with Sundays. Most of the existing scholarship on the Byzantine liturgical year comes from the field of comparative liturgy. These historical works are essential. The church adjusts to contemporary conditions by digging deeply into history, which allows it to come to terms with the past and arrive at an understanding that enables true worship in the present.

This book is rooted in and attempts to honor the scholarship of the heavyweights of Byzantine liturgical history. Its objective is to engage readers in a discussion on the meaning of the liturgical year in its present form by looking at its primary seasons and feasts. It does so by exploring history and the primary liturgical components of word, rite, and song. Much of the analysis delves into the significance of the lectionary as the primary source of liturgical theology, but it gives due consideration to primary rites as well. The appointed hymns are, of course, important, and readers will notice that hymns are included as key sources of analysis but not privileged over the other sources. This falls in accordance with one of the primary rules of the method of liturgical theology, which is to respect the liturgy as an act and event. Liturgy is neither a text nor a song, even though euchology and hymnography rank high among the sources for liturgical theology.

If the study's objective is to make sense of the liturgical year as it truly is, then it has the potential to identify problems. It both does so and offers potential resolutions. With the objective of being brutally honest about findings, it is guided by the belief that naming a problem empowers practitioners to resolve it. The suggestions proposed here are designed to be dialogical—let pastors decide the best course of action for their people.

Acknowledgments

M OST BOOKS INCLUDE A section with thanks conveyed to a long list of the author's interlocutors. Readers may be surprised by the brevity and unconventional form of the current list. There are two reasons for the particular structure of this section. The first is deeply personal. This book was in progress with a viable plan for completion until a life-changing event took place when my wife, Tresja, died suddenly and unexpectedly. After a necessary pause, I adjusted my plans, resumed the project, and completed the manuscript.

As for acknowledgments, there are a few. This book has many sources of inspiration. Most of those come from my own experiences of the liturgical year as both a choir director and a deacon. The first time I ever conducted a choir was in 1991 at St. Volodymyr and Ol'ha Ukrainian Orthodox Parish in St. Paul, Minnesota. I led the singing for the midnight paschal services. Pascha happened to coincide with the Annunciation that year. So, the first service I was to lead happened to be a rare occurrence on the calendar—Kyriopascha, a dual feast calling for singing that would take a parish from midnight to sunrise and possibly beyond. The pastor—my grandfather—decided to scale back the number of Annunciation hymns required by the Typikon to keep the service manageable. That occasion was my first experience of the many twists and turns in the Orthodox liturgical year, one that always generated many more questions than answers.

Over the years, conversations with countless clergy heightened my sense of urgency to pursue a better understanding of the church year. I simply cannot include everyone, so I apologize for the omissions, but my interlocutors over the years include Kira Tsarehradsky, my mentor in choral conducting, and several clergy and faithful of numerous Orthodox communities: Fathers Vladimir Lecko (of blessed memory), Ted Wojcik, Brian Andrew Jaye, Jonathan Proctor, Paul Lazor (of blessed memory), Steve Salaris, Lawrence Gaudreau, Constantine White, Sergius Miller (of blessed memory), Ray Velencia, Duane Johnson, Yousuf Rassam, Michael Courey, Jacob van Sickle, William Mills, Michael Plekon, Alexis Vinogradov, Daniel Galadza, Stavros Winner, Heorhiy Kovalenko, and Andriy Dudchenko. There have also been countless conversations with David Drillock, Andrew Lukashonak, Kevin Smith, Adam DeVille, and Teva Regule. I am especially grateful to Michael Plekon and Mark Roosien for providing feedback on the initial manuscript draft. I am grateful to them for the constant exchange of ideas and fraternal dialogue in Christ. I also thank the sponsoring editor of this volume, Matthew Wimer, and Julie Lind for copy editing. Last, personal thanks to Sophia and Greg for support and encouragement.

Finally, my preface mentions the "other" side of communal feasts. The study and discussion of feasts tends to idealize community gatherings with the reverent language of peace, tranquility, and fellowship. Feasts include these elements, but they also have the other human side. Celebrants and choirs make liturgical mistakes. Pastors miscommunicate the message of the feast. People misbehave and alienate one another. Try as we may, we cannot get in God's way. At every feast, God is with us, and nothing can stop God from making God's dwelling among us. It is for this reason that the liturgical year always has been and always will be a source of joy for Christians.

1

Introducing the Liturgical Year

C ELEBRATING THE LITURGICAL YEAR in the Orthodox Church is
  eventful. Orthodoxy shares many feasts with the churches of the
West. Lent, Holy Week, Pascha (Easter), and Pentecost are among the most
solemn seasons and days. Orthodoxy also has many Marian feasts, similar to the Roman Catholic liturgical tradition. Mary's Birth, Entrance into
the Temple, Annunciation, and Dormition (Assumption) occupy central
places on the church calendar.

The particularities of the Orthodox calendar are easily explained by
liturgical history. Lent begins with a special Vespers office on the Sunday
evening before the Monday of the first week. There is no Ash Wednesday
in Orthodoxy—this rite is particular to the West, a regional tradition
that the churches of the East neither experienced nor received. Similarly,
though the Sundays of Advent are central to the Western Christian celebration of Christmas, there is no official Advent in Orthodoxy, but there
is a forty-day fast preceding Christmas, along with two preparatory Sundays. Theophany (Epiphany) is a festive occasion in Orthodoxy, featuring
the blessing of waters, which the faithful then take home to be consumed
for protection, healing, and the forgiveness of sins. This short description
of differences between the Orthodox and Roman Catholic Church barely
breaks the surface—the Orthodox liturgical year contains many more
mysteries to be explored.

This Study's Objective

There is a plethora of scholarship on the liturgical year in Orthodoxy. A cad-
re of first-rate comparative liturgists has delivered numerous monographs

and articles explaining the historical development of specific feasts, fasts, and seasons. Much of the scholarship is devoted to Holy Week and Pascha. The editions of the late-antique to medieval Armenian and Georgian lectionaries provide insights into the celebration of the entire liturgical year in Jerusalem. The editions compiled, translated, and published by scholars such as Athanase Renoux and Michel Tarchnischvili remain necessary for the study of this early period of liturgical history. The so-called Anastasis typikon provides details on hagiopolite Holy Week and Pascha in the tenth century. The editions of the Typikon of the Great Church published by Juan Mateos reveal the Constantinopolitan cursus of services.

Several scholars have contributed to an ongoing narrative on the details of Holy Week and Pascha. These studies include Mark Morozowich's detailed analysis of Holy Thursday, Sebastia Janeras's study of Holy Friday, and Gabriel Bertonière's history of the Paschal Vigil.[1] In addition, Miguel Arranz has written multiple essays on paschal baptism and the kneeling prayers at Pentecost, Robert Taft has an analysis of the cross-pollination of Jerusalem and Constantinople during Holy Week and Pascha, Thomas Pott has examined the Paschal Triduum, and Daniel Galadza has produced a groundbreaking study of liturgical Byzantinization in Jerusalem.

General studies on the origins of the liturgical year are informative. Paul Bradshaw and Maxwell Johnson's survey of the historical development of feasts, fasts, and seasons reflects on many issues relevant to the Orthodox tradition. The significance of Lazarus Saturday in the period bridging Lent and Holy Week is of particular interest and updates the previous scholarship of Thomas Talley. A number of important questions on the objectives of studying the liturgical year have surfaced in the academic community. These are summarized in an important survey essay by Harald Buchinger, who discloses the existing questions on certain assumptions such as the origins of the Christmas feast and the role of the interplay of theory and practice in the history of the liturgical year.[2] The most important study written for a general audience on the Orthodox liturgical year is Archbishop Job Getcha's exposition of the typikon, published originally in French and now translated in English.[3] Getcha's study analyzes

---

1. Morozowich, *Holy Thursday*; Janeras, *La Vendredi-Saint*; Bertonière, *Historical Development*; Pott, *Byzantine Liturgical Reform*; Galadza, *Liturgy and Byzantinization*; Taft, "Holy Week"; Taft, "In the Bridegroom's."

2. Buchinger, "On the Origin."

3. Getcha, *Typikon Decoded*.

the intersecting liturgical cycles through the lens of the liturgical books. His presentation explains the overarching system that pastors find in the typikon, including the categorization of feasts through their symbols and the historical development of the liturgical books that provide the content for the offices of the church year. Getcha's study is particularly valuable for its digests of historical evolution and descriptions of the primary features of the liturgical year. He covers Lent, Holy Week, Pascha, the Ascension, Pentecost, Christmas, and the Theophany.

A selection of other publications offers reflections on the liturgical year. These include Alexander Schmemann's essays on Great Lent, Thomas Hopko's collections on the Christmas and Lenten seasons, Lev Gillet's meditation on the church year, and Alkiviadis Calivas's important introduction to Holy Week and Pascha in the Greek Orthodox tradition.[4]

This book's objectives are as follows: First, this study surveys the received liturgical tradition and considers the present realities of its celebration in the Orthodox Church. The examination of each ritual celebration is irreducible to any single festal feature. The relationship of the liturgical year with the calendar can lead to the impression that the significance of a feast depends largely on its position within the structures and rhythms of seasons. This study will show that the liturgical year is irreducible to the governance of time and the interpretations of dates and numbers.

In this sense, the study does not seek to reveal the origins of the feasts or reconstruct their historical development, though each section will discuss history's contribution to our understanding of feasts. The book approaches Orthodoxy's celebration of the liturgical year as it is in the present. We explain the meaning of each celebration by accounting for all festal components. For most feasts and ritual acts, the order of the cycle of services, appointed scriptural lessons, hymns, and special ritual actions are the primary components for defining its meaning. The methodology of this book follows the principle elucidated by Mark Searle, who described the liturgical year as "a carousel of sayings and stories, songs and prayers, processions and silences, images and visions, symbols and rituals, feasts and fasts in which the mysterious ways of God are not merely presented but experienced, not merely perused but lived through."[5]

---

4. Schmemann, *Great Lent*; Hopko, *Winter Pascha* and *Lenten Spring*; Calivas, *Great Week and Pascha*; A Monk of the Eastern Church, *Year of Grace*. "A Monk of the Eastern Church" is a pseudonym occasionally used by Lev Gillet.

5. Searle, "Sunday," 59.

In Orthodoxy, festal hymnography occupies a place of prominence in expressing liturgical theology. Hymns are regarded as the living repository of patristic preaching, the continued echoing of the voice of the fathers in the contemporary church. This study devotes more energy to gleaning liturgical theology from the appointed scriptural lessons to clarify the meaning of any given feast.

Ordering the Liturgical Year

This analysis of the liturgical year does not follow a chronological order. We do not begin on September 1 (the Indiction) and proceed to the end of August. Rather, this survey has a thematic organization. The first content chapter covers the movable cycle, Pascha and the seasons and commemorations that depend on the calculation of its annual date. It provides a detailed analysis of the pre-Lenten cycle of Sundays, Lent, Holy Week, Pascha, and the Ascension and Pentecost. The discussion of the commemorations included in the movable cycle includes the Sundays honoring ecumenical councils and All Saints Sunday. The next chapter presents the fixed cycle of the liturgical year and focuses on the feasts of the Lord and Marian commemorations. The analysis begins with the cycle of incarnational feasts—Christmas, the Theophany, and Hypapante (Meeting). The chapter proceeds on to an analysis of the Marian cycle (the four Great Feasts), a discussion of the commemorations of John the Baptist, and a section on two stand-alone, fixed feasts of the Lord—the Transfiguration and the Exaltation of the Cross. The last content chapter covers "everything else," including a discussion of the veneration of the saints followed by a description of a selection of prevalent icon feasts. The analysis of this chapter addresses the occasionally thorny relationship between sanctorals and ideology, especially when church communities use beloved national saints or historical events as platforms for promulgating ideological agendas. Themes expressed in the services of St. Job of Pochaiv, the Baptism of Rus', and St. John Maximovich are the examples explored here. The section on icon feasts discusses the real inspiration for these holidays—modern epiphanies through icons and relics—and ethical issues related to the church's tendency to use miraculous icons to recruit new members.

One aspect of the liturgical year that warrants much more academic and pastoral analysis is the presence of a number of domestic traditions associated with feasts. Orthodox members throughout the world practice rituals that represent the life of the church in the home. The last chapter orients readers to the significance of such domestic practices by surveying three well-known traditions: the Serbian *Krsna Slava* (patron saint celebration); the *Sviata Vechera* (Holy Supper) observance common to Ukrainians, Belarussians, Carpatho-Rusyns, and Poles; and the annual baking of the savory *Vasilopita* in honor of St. Basil on January 1 among Greeks.

Discussion of Problems and Opportunities

An engaged discussion of the challenges posed to the church by the liturgical year takes place in the penultimate chapter of this book. The unique history of the Orthodox Church has constrained the freedom of church leaders to meet regularly and deliberate on pressing issues. Many liturgical reforms have been implemented but not universally and only in certain local churches.

The reality is that pastors have inherited a largely unedited tradition. On the one hand, the sheer volume of content—the calendar has countless saints, and their feasts often coincide with one another—provides opportunities to share the life of a new saint or epiphany with the faithful. On the other hand, the absence of a sustained stewardship of the liturgy and the sources that govern the rhythm of the liturgical year frequently requires pastors to make decisions on content when the rubrics call for multiple commemorations or rigorous liturgical cycles.

Pastors navigate the complexities of the liturgical year in diverse ways that can be described by two broad schools of thought.[6] The first regards the received tradition as the natural outcome of organic historical development, a sacred tradition that prohibits change. This approach encourages pastors to exhort the people to engage the liturgy as it is and, in so doing, to change the culture. The other approach views the liturgy as constantly evolving through the vicissitudes of time and culture in the spirit of *ecclesia reformanda semper*. This views the typikon that governs the distribution of content as providing an ideal pattern that pastors consult and adapt to the realities of their community's life.[7] This is not so much the adaptation of the liturgy to the prevailing culture as it is an honoring of the core of the pattern without the obligation of adopting every detail. Here, I

6. Pott's discussion of the approaches of *Sacrosanctum Concilium* and *Orientalium Ecclesiarum* apply here in Pott, *Byzantine Liturgical Reform*, 43–46.

7. On the typikon as a pattern, see Larin, "Feasting and Fasting."

raise the issue of pastoral interpretations of the concept of the typikon to magnify the real challenges the liturgical year occasionally poses to pastors. These issues are especially prevalent during the most solemn seasons: Holy Week, Pascha, and Christmas. Pastors who want to observe the established pattern without adaptation will find themselves in church every day. Observing this order is difficult for the standard parish community with one choral or music leader and a handful of singers.

A tendency has taken shape in Western Orthodox culture that defines Holy Week as a progression leading up to Pascha as the destination of the journey. The same principle applies to the shorter but still intense cycle of Christmas services. The Hours, Vesperal Liturgy, and Vigil precede the Divine Liturgy on Christmas morning as the end of the journey. In some instances, pastors instruct people to use vacation time to attend all of the services and—more importantly for our purposes—define participation in the entire cycle as necessary, singling out one of the services as the summit of the liturgical journey. A discussion about the inner synergy of the festal cycle and the expectations for participation is the first of a handful of problems and opportunities discussed in the penultimate chapter. The rest of the chapter is devoted to three distinct problems. The first is the exploitation of feasts to promote spurious ideological platforms or recirculate polemical tropes expressed by the hymnography. The next is the temptation to commodify icon feasts and the reproduction of relics. Third is the question of time in the liturgical year.

The sheer volume of hymnography appointed to feasts and the impact of the multiple messages proclaimed in hymns on people's cognitive capacity is a difficult issue because of the church's veneration for the hymnographical tradition. The analysis suggests a review of the corpus of hymnography so that the songs that proclaim the Orthodox theology of feasts are able to be heard, learned, and received in the minds and hearts of the faithful.

Scholars and theologians have naturally associated the liturgical year with the human experience and meaning of time. Early scholarship considered the classic relationship between kairos and chronos. Liturgical scholars incorporated the analysis of time, the liturgical year, and the Liturgy of the Hours into the sanctification of time and the symbiosis of the past, the present, and the future in the liturgy. The section on time emphasizes the contributions of Robert Taft and Matias Augé, who described the liturgical year as a spiral progressing toward the parousia.[8] We also present the important perspective of Lizette Larson-Miller, who argues for the retention of concrete festal gatherings as a Christian response to the crisis of the commodification of time.[9]

The chapter concludes with our assessment of the question of time. The energy devoted to developing scholarship on this matter was necessary, but, in the process, the assumption emerged that the liturgical year is all about time. This study suggests that the power of community memory is the core energy cell of the liturgical year. When the power of community memory becomes traditional—passed on from one generation to the next—it enables anamnesis to lead organically to epiclesis so that every generation receives the blessings of the feast. This study asserts that the liturgical year can be experienced and comprehended more effectively when appraised from the lens of community memory.

Sources for the Celebration of the Liturgical Year

Pastors and musicians need to be competent in navigating a selection of books and related sources for celebrating the feasts of the liturgical year. The primary book scholars and pastors refer to—somewhat informally—is called the typikon. It originated as a written rule for monastic communities and became associated with liturgics when monasteries added the particular details for their community's liturgical celebration to the monastic rule. In everyday Church parlance, it is a book that lists the appointed psalmody, Bible readings, the order of hymns, saints commemorated, and any other special ritual instructions. It refers to multiple iterations, not one master source used by all Orthodox communities. Rather, each local church publishes its own version of a typikon on an annual basis to guide parish observance of the liturgical year. No two typika are identical since history led to minor regional differences in the celebration of certain offices, and each church has its own list of local saints. The typikon provides a summary and does not include the entire texts of readings or hymns. It is a guide used by pastors and musicians who consult other related sources for the performance of the celebration.

8. Augé, "Theology," 322; Taft, *Beyond East and West*, 15–30.
9. Larson-Miller, "Consuming Time."

An example of a master typikon is one published by the Moscow Patriarchate (Russian Orthodox Church).[10] This typikon follows the established order of rules that address issues ranging from etiquette (when to cover one's head) to the times appointed for silence during meals. The instructions for observing the liturgical year occupy only a few chapters but also compose most of the content. This study occasionally refers to this particular master typikon when discussing certain festal liturgical components and issues.

Festal Types

The Moscow typikon was designed to be a helpful guide. It includes the numbers assigned to the specific Gospel readings, allowing priests, deacons, and lectors to search for and find the reading. The typikon also includes a kind of categorization of festal celebrations indicated by specific markings or signs adjacent to the corresponding date.[11] These signs alert liturgical participants to the kind of feast they are celebrating. An encircled cross designates great feasts of Christ, Mary, two of John the Baptist, and the feast of the apostles Peter and Paul. A cross with a circle on the bottom half designates middle feasts that include a vigil with a canon to the Theotokos. Readers seeking more detailed information should consult Getcha's description of the signs used in the Slavic and Greek versions of the typikon.[12] He states that the categorizations reveal the degrees of solemnity and the shape of the office to be celebrated.

Four books are essential for the Orthodox celebration of the liturgical year: the Octoechos, Menaion, Triodion, and Pentecostarion. The Octoechos provides the hymns for each Sunday.[13] The word refers to the system of eight modes assigned to each Sunday and its corresponding week throughout the year. The Octoechos forms the basis for Sunday singing. Its repetition throughout the year makes it memorable, so communities are familiar with the hymns repeated every eight weeks. It contains the complete texts of the appointed hymns for cantors and choirs. The Menaion contains the instructions and texts needed for the celebrations of the fixed cycle of the liturgical year. This study relies upon the English

---

10. *Тѷпїконъ сіестъ уставъ.* "Typikon" hereafter.

11. Typikon, 107–8.

12. Getcha, *Typikon Decoded*, 99.

13. See *The Great Octoechos* for an English translation.

translation of *The Festal Menaion* by Kallistos Ware and Mother Mary, widely known and circulated among Anglophone Orthodox communities.[14] Ware and Mother Mary also translated and compiled an extensive English translation of *The Lenten Triodion*.[15] This book contains the propers and hymns for the Lenten services, beginning with the Sunday of the Publican and the Pharisee of the pre-Lenten period and up until the end of the Paschal Vigil (also known as the Vespers and Liturgy of Holy Saturday). The Pentecostarion covers the liturgical content for Pascha through the first Sunday after Pentecost (All Saints).[16] The method and objective for using this book is the same as the others.

Practical Sources for Exercise of the Ministry

In practice, parishes do not use these sources for liturgical celebration. Numerous publications and translations are available online. Local churches provide resources for parishes to execute the office of the liturgical year. The Greek Orthodox Archdiocese of America maintains an online digital chant stand providing convenient access of the required texts and hymns to pastors and musicians.[17] This resource serves the needs of the archdiocese by providing both text and musical settings in English and Greek. The Orthodox Church in America provides a similar online service by publishing on its website the necessary liturgical texts for each Sunday and some major feasts.

Local churches also publish convenient offprints of specific feasts, cycles, or individual services of the liturgical year. For example, the Greek Orthodox Archdiocese has one book containing the texts for Holy Week and Pascha in bilingual format. The primary books of the liturgical year have been repackaged into a variety of print and online sources that are more convenient for users. The four primary sources are necessary reference tools, and practitioners have redistributed them into user-friendly, pocket-sized service books and downloadable online documents.

The result of this necessary repackaging is the presence of multiple translations of texts and varying musical settings in print and online. Pastors and musicians have many options when searching for sources for the

14. *Festal Menaion.*
15. *Lenten Triodion.*
16. This study uses *The Pentecostarion*, rev. 2nd ed.
17. Digital Chant Stand.

liturgical year. This study does not account for all of the extant English translations of the four primary sources. It notes that practitioners use diverse sources to perform their ministries for the services, and the study itself relies on the English translations by Ware, Mother Mary, and the monastics of the Holy Transfiguration Monastery.

The ultimate purpose of this book is to glean meaning from the established ritual celebration of the liturgical year. Readers will discover that the liturgical year was inspired by sacred topography and experienced significant expansion into a complex system of feasts and rubrics. The church has chosen to attempt to manage the complexity of the system by appointing a variety of combinations of commemorations, themes, and hymns. Occasionally, the festal complexity creates confusion, and this study offers suggestions for purifying aspects of the festal mechanism to grant the faithful access to clear meaning. Despite the challenges posed by the accumulation of material throughout history, it is the core meaning of the feasts that continues to vivify their celebration and inspire the faithful to assemble on the appointed dates. One message cuts through the sheer volume of material and makes the liturgical year an extraordinary experience for participants: God is with his people, and the feasts renew and deepen their fellowship with God and the community of saints.

2

The Movable Cycle

T HE ORDINARY ORTHODOX CHRISTIAN anticipates Pascha more than any other feast of the liturgical year. The famous canon written by St. John of Damascus, sung at Paschal Matins, describes Pascha as "the chosen and holy day" and the "feast of feasts."[1] While the authors of the hymns for other feasts use similar language, Pascha is the heart of the Orthodox liturgical year. The calculation of the date for Pascha is the heart of the movable cycle, as this date governs the Sundays and weeks of the Lenten and pentecostarion commemorations.[2] In fact, Pascha dictates the rhythm for most of any given liturgical year, since the Sundays after Pentecost—the Orthodox sibling of "Ordinary Time" in the Western Christian tradition—depend on the timing of Pascha itself.

This chapter presents the history, key ritual features, and theology of the movable cycle of the liturgical year in Orthodoxy. The presentation begins with the preparatory period, or Sundays before Lent, and continues with an examination of Lent, Holy Week, Pascha, the Sundays of Pascha, the Ascension, Pentecost, and All Saints Sunday.

---

1. Contos, *Services for Holy Week*, 570–71.

2. An analysis of the historical development of Easter in the early church and methods for the calculation of the date of Pascha is outside of this study's scope. For an evaluation of the Orthodox calculation method, see Fotopoulos, "Some Common." For a serious attempt to arrive at a new ecumenical consensus on the date of Pascha, see World Council of Churches, "Towards a Common Date for Easter," also known as the Aleppo Statement of the World Council of Churches in 1997. For a critical survey of scholarship on the origins of Easter, see Buchinger, "On the Origin," 18–21.

The Preparatory Sundays of Lent

Currently, the five Sundays preceding Lent function as preparatory Sundays.[3] These Sundays are based on the appointed Gospel lessons and include Zacchaeus Sunday (or the Canaanite Woman), the Publican and the Pharisee, the Prodigal Son, Meatfare / Last Judgment, and Cheesefare / the Expulsion of Adam and Eve from Paradise.

Table 2.1: Commemorations and Readings of Pre-Lenten Sundays

Preparatory Sunday	Gospel Lesson
Zacchaeus (Sl.) / Canaanite Woman (Gr.)	Luke 19:1–10, Matt 15:21–28 (Gr.)
Publican and Pharisee (Triodion begins)	Luke 18:10–14
Prodigal Son	Luke 15:11–32
Meatfare / Last Judgment	Matt 25:31–46
Cheesefare / Expulsion of Adam and Eve	Matt 6:4–14

There is a discrepancy among the Orthodox churches on the current order of pre-Lenten Sundays. Among the Slavic churches, Zacchaeus Sunday provides the first cue for the beginning of this period.[4] In the churches of the Greek tradition, the Sunday of the Canaanite Woman begins the rather lengthy preparatory period. There seems to be some minor disagreement within the church on the exact beginning of this period; singing from the triodion, or Lenten hymnal, begins on the Sunday of the Publican and Pharisee. It has become customary for clergy and insiders to greet one another with "a blessed triodion to you" as a way of marking the pre-Lenten season. These discrepancies and the importance assigned to the Sunday that inaugurates the preparatory season demonstrates the solemnity of the preparatory period among Orthodox Christians.

Historically, the current arrangement and order of the preparatory Sundays seems to be the result of some shuffling of the Sundays and their respective commemorations. The Typikon of the Great Church appoints the readings for the Prodigal Son to the Sunday before the Meatfare.[5] The

3. The texts and order of services for the preparatory Sundays of the Triodion are taken from *Lenten Triodion*, 99–188.

4. See Schmemann, *Great Lent*, 17.

5. Mateos, "Cycle des fetes mobiles," 2–3. See the overview on the configuration of

Sundays of Judgment and Cheesefare follow, but the list that begins the Constantinopolitan pre-Lenten period excludes mention of the Publican and Pharisee, Zacchaeus, and the Canaanite Woman. The Constantinopolitan tradition appoints the readings for Zacchaeus to the thirty-first Sunday, the Canaanite Woman to the thirty-second, and the Publican and Pharisee to the thirty-third, at the end of the movable cycle and the Sundays after Pentecost.[6]

As the Orthodox liturgy evolved and the appointed lessons were rearranged in local lectionaries, the Gospels for Zacchaeus and the Canaanite Woman appeared in various orders. Constantinople's designation of the Prodigal Son readings to the Sunday before the Meatfare illustrates the designation of the Lenten preparatory period for the imperial capital. As the Orthodox liturgy evolved through the cross-pollination of cathedral and monastic liturgical traditions, the designation of the beginning of the preparatory period changed. The stewards of the liturgical tradition folded the commemoration of the thirty-third Sunday (Publican and Pharisee) into the pre-Lenten period.[7] In the received tradition, that period technically commences as the church begins to use the Lenten hymnal (triodion).

The migration of readings and commemorations assigned to the pre-Lenten Sundays from one position to another is a customary characteristic of liturgical evolution. While this pattern is a bit confusing, it conforms to the larger blueprint of Byzantine liturgical history that consists of cross-pollination among the monastic and cathedral centers in Jerusalem and Constantinople and the eventual establishment of a type of synthesis that continues to function in the received tradition.

The meaning and liturgical experience of the pre-Lenten preparatory period is much more significant for our purposes. The sequence of Sundays functions as a gradual immersion into the period of Lent. The preparatory period introduces the core concepts and habits that ideally become part of the community's daily Lenten habit. The primary themes are humility and repentance, and the habits are to adopt the identities of sinner and penitent and to gradually begin the practice of fasting.

---

readings appointed to these Sundays in Bertonière, *Sundays of Lent,* 30–32.

6. Mateos, "Cycle des fetes mobiles," 166–67.

7. See Getcha, *Typikon Decoded,* 141–42.

Introducing Fasting a la Orthodoxy

The preparatory period begins with a rather drastic change in diet in an un-expected direction. The week after the Sunday of the Publican and Pharisee is fast-free, which means that the Orthodox are exempt from the customary fast appointed to Wednesdays and Fridays of most weeks. While the reasons for this fast are spurious because of their polemical origins, the result is pleasant for those who observe the weekly regimen of two strict days.[8] There is no parallel observance of Mardi Gras, or Fat Tuesday, in Orthodox culture, so this fast-free week probably comes closest to capturing the spirit of pre-Lenten feasting among the people.

The actual introduction to the habit of fasting for the Orthodox occurs on Meatfare Sunday, the last day for eating meat until Pascha. Dairy, olive oil, and wine are permitted for the final week before Lent begins, known as Cheesefare week. This week shares one similarity with the week following the Publican and Pharisee; the abstention from cheese, eggs, olive oil, and wine is lifted on Wednesday and Friday. A culture of feasting has emerged in the time around this week. Eastern Slavic people celebrate *Maslenitsa*, a celebration that features dairy-based foods and often includes formal banquets and dances.[9] The final dairy-based meal takes place on Cheesefare Sunday, until the strict Lenten rules for fasting begin on the Monday of Clean Week.

Ritual Components of Pre-Lent

The pre-Lenten period introduces new ritual components. "Open unto Me," a hymn of repentance, is added to the Sunday Matins service.[10] This hymn occurs after the Gospel lesson, within the structure of the verses of Psalm 51 customarily appointed. The hymn of repentance begins on this first Sunday of the pre-Lenten period and remains in place throughout the Sundays of Great Lent.

The singing of Psalm 137 is added to the Sunday Matins service on the Sunday of the Prodigal Son, the second Sunday of this period.[11] This

8. For the historical origins of the polemical justification for a fast-free week, see Getcha, *Typikon Decoded*, 142–43.

9. For background on the complete history of this holiday, see Riabkov, "Maslenitsa."

10. *Lenten Triodion*, 101.

11. *Lenten Triodion*, 114.

addition is similar to the hymn of repentance on the previous Sunday, as it occurs before the Gospel and after the usual singing of Psalm 136. There is one difference in the rubrics: the hymn of repentance remains in place throughout Great Lent, whereas Psalm 137 is taken through the Matins of Cheesefare Sunday. Psalm 137, then, is assigned only to the Lenten preparatory period.

In parish practice, the singing of the hymn of repentance and Psalm 137 is the most prominent feature of the preparatory period, outside of the Sunday Gospels. These two liturgical components take place during Matins, a service that is not well attended by the people. Pastors instruct choirs and chanters to sing the two hymns during the preparation of Holy Communion and while people are venerating the cross and receiving antidoron at the Sunday Divine Liturgy. These hymns are well known, popular among the people, and have numerous musical settings for choirs. Both hymns are also sung throughout Lent itself, even though Psalm 137 is appointed to the preparatory period. Technically, the hymn and psalm are not suitable for the time before receiving Holy Communion. Their popularity among the people supersedes any sense of incompatibility with preparation for Holy Communion.

The Gospels of the Preparatory Period

The appointed Gospel lessons for the preparatory Sundays are the primary sources for their liturgical theology. The first two Sundays feature parables from the Gospel of Luke and the two overarching themes of Lent itself: humility and repentance. On both occasions, the Gospel invites the faithful to adopt the identity of flawed characters. In the first parable, the Pharisee appears to be righteous because of his deeds, whereas the Publican's occupation casts doubt on his character. Yet it is the Publican who exemplifies Christian humility. He confesses his own sin and asks for forgiveness and mercy without calling attention to his neighbor. The account presents the Pharisee as the model to be avoided, as the story reveals his apparent outward piety to be false, since his inner life is puffed up with pride. This simple, fundamental lesson teaches the faithful to concentrate on confessing their own sins without comparing themselves to others.

The second parable on the prodigal son features the younger child, who wastes his inheritance only to realize his error and request clemency from his father. This story presents three images, two favorable and one to be avoided. The young prodigal is the penitent, the one who squanders what he has been given only to return home, empty-handed and humbled. His father is the head of the household who receives him with joy and refrains from punishing him for wasting his inheritance. The point is simple, profound, and stands at the center of Christian life. Christians fail and waste the gifts they have received from God. Acknowledging failure and returning home brings amnesty even when one returns empty-handed.

The prodigal son parable introduces the third character, the older brother who is his father's loyal servant. The older brother's complaint about the father's joyous reception of the prodigal son repeats the theme of refraining from judging others introduced on the first Sunday. The older brother is like the Pharisee—outwardly righteous and expecting a reward for his loyalty. Inwardly, he is filled with pride and wants the father to reward him for his loyalty. The joyous reception of the prodigal son ignites envy in the older brother. The faithful are called to be like the prodigal in acknowledging their own faults and having the courage to return home with the knowledge that they will be received joyfully. The readings present an image of God who rejoices over the return of the sinner.

The two parables are not limited to the tropological models depicted by the characters, however. They initiate the hearers of the word into habits of acknowledging their own sins and learning how to confess and return to God without comparing their virtues and vices with others in the community. Essentially, the first two Sundays in this preparatory period begin the process of initiating the faithful into an order of penitents. The Christian faithful become students of humility and penitence.

Second Stage of Initiation: Judgment and Forgiveness

The titles for the two Sundays preceding Lent—Meatfare and Cheesefare—emphasize the forthcoming period of fasting. As the primary sources of liturgical theology, the two Gospel lessons assigned to these Sundays reveal the inner meaning of liturgical participation. These two Sundays complete the initiation of the faithful into the order of penitents by preparing them for judgment and exhorting them to forgive and receive forgiveness.

The other title for Meatfare Sunday is the Last Judgment. This Sunday features the Matthean Gospel lesson in which Jesus promises paradise for those who attend to the least of his brethren and warns of damnation for those who ignore them. The hymnography accompanying the Gospel lesson is vivid in its dire warnings of the penalties to be assigned to those who ignore the least of the brethren. The faithful hear of rivers of fire that will burn and devour and of the saints who enjoy paradise and the sinners falling into the pit of fire in the iconography.[12] This Sunday reminds the faithful that Christian life is communal and that attending to one's own private spiritual life is not enough; one must also partake in the sacrament of the brother and sister by attending to the least of the Lord's brethren, which is the preferred manner of demonstrating love for God. It is also a stern and necessary reminder that the Christian life is not confined to the present but is oriented toward the future, where one lives in community with Christ—and the least of his brethren.

Like the first two Sundays in this series, the final preparatory Sunday completes the themes introduced by the Last Judgment by emphasizing forgiveness. It contains three themes—fasting (Cheesefare), the expulsion of Adam and Eve from paradise, and forgiveness. The expulsion and forgiveness themes work together. The Matthean Gospel exhorts hearers of the commandment to forgive. The recurring theme of the accompanying hymnography is of Adam, cast out of Eden and crying "woe is me."[13] The faithful who hear this Gospel know that Christ has opened paradise to all through his cross—a message of the hymnography appointed to the third Sunday of Lent, the one of the cross. Receiving and imparting forgiveness does not come easily—it requires the humility, confession of one's own sin, and care for the least of the Lord's brethren introduced by the first three preparatory Sundays. The Gospel lesson emphasizes that asking for God's forgiveness is not enough—it is also necessary to again participate in the sacrament of the brother and sister by forgiving all others. Imparting and receiving forgiveness heals broken communities. These are acts of allowing pride, envy, bitterness, and division to die or, better yet, to allow Christ to crucify them by his cross. As with the previous Sunday, forgiveness is the path to ending woes and restoring communion—again, with Christ and with the least of his brethren.

Two observations conclude this review of the prominent Lenten preparatory period. First, the themes of the period remind the faithful that the future life of eternity is neither distant nor separated from present experience. It is the future of life shared with God and the community of the least of his brethren that shapes the necessity and urgency of adopting Christian

12. See the first sticheron of Vespers in *Lenten Triodion*, 150.

13. The hymns contain multiple cries of "woe is me." See *Lenten Triodion*, 169.

humility, the acknowledgment of sin, and the desire to return home in the present. The commemorations of the preparatory Sundays look forward as much as they look back to the past. Second, the preparatory period expanded from two Sundays previewing Lent to four, with the triodion also beginning on the first Sunday. Historically, the gradual liturgical monastic and cathedral synthesis caused the expansion of the pre-Lenten period. It is essentially the result of the organic development of liturgy. This expansion enhanced the solemnity of the preparatory period. It is almost as long as Lent itself, and it includes one week of limited fasting. The increased prominence of the Lenten preparatory period represents the solemnity of Lent itself. The observance of Lent was so important in the life of the church that it slowly created an entirely new season of preparation. This chapter has identified the Sunday Gospel lessons as the primary sources for the liturgical theology of the preparatory period. Ironically, these Gospels are more Lenten in character than those assigned to Lent itself, a matter to which we will return in our concluding reflections.

Lent: History and a Sketch

The twentieth-century liturgical movement encouraged scholars and pastors to return to the sources. Historical research illuminated Lent as a time of intense preparation for baptism, evidenced by the catechetical lectures of pastors and new information on other liturgical components. Students of liturgy began to view Lent as a preparation for baptism on Pascha.[14] Many clergy and faithful continued to view Lent as a penitential season of preparation for Pascha.

Liturgical historians have recently demonstrated that Lent comes in a variety of shapes and sizes, depending largely on regional Christian traditions.[15] In the second century, Christians from Asia Minor observed a one-day strict fast that culminated with a long vigil commemorating the life of Christ, from his incarnation through his resurrection.[16] In other places, Lent was observed for three weeks. By the fourth century, Lent

14. See, for example, Schmemann, *Great Lent,* 14. See also Johnson, *Rites of Christian Initiation,* 159–76, and Buchinger, "On the Origin," 44.

15. For a summary of the status of the question, see Bradshaw and Johnson, *Origins of Feasts,* 99–108.

16. Bradshaw and Johnson, *Origins of Feasts,* 43–44. See also Stewart-Sykes, *Melito of Sardis* for an English translation of the text.

became associated with forty days. The Alexandrian Church features a forty-day fast in imitation of Jesus' forty days in the wilderness, devoted to intense prayer.[17] The order of this particular model is noteworthy: the Holy Spirit leads Jesus into the desert for an intense forty-day fast immediately following his baptism.[18]

While the scholarship on the history of Lent reveals diverse calculations and observances in early Christianity, Lent is essentially standardized for today's Orthodox Church. Table 2.2 depicts the Sundays and weeks of Lent along with their primary themes.

Table 2.2: Sundays and Weeks of Lent

Sunday	Gospel	Commemorations, Theme	Weekly Liturgical Components
Sunday night Forgiveness Vespers		Forgiveness, Clean Week	Canon of St. Andrew of Crete
1. Triumph of Orthodoxy	John 1		Liturgy of Presanctified Gifts

Memorial divine liturgies are celebrated on the second, third, and fourth Saturdays of Lent.

2. St. Gregory Palamas	Mark		Liturgy of Presanctified Gifts
3. The Cross	Mark	The cross	Liturgy of Presanctified Gifts / Veneration of the cross
4. St. John Climacus	Mark		Liturgy of Presanctified Gifts / Prayers for photizomenoi[19]

Fifth Saturday of Lent: Akathistos Hymn (observed on Friday evening)

17. Note the contentious scholarly debate on this matter summarized by Bradshaw and Johnson, *Origins of Feasts*, 100–107. See also Russo, "Origins of Lent," 126–49.

18. Russo, "Origins of Lent," 106–7.

19. "Photizomenoi" means "those who will be illuminated" and refers to an order of catechumens who are in the final stages of preparation for baptism. The church intensifies prayer for those in this last stage.

5. St. Mary of Egypt	Mark		Canon of St. Andrew of Crete / Vita of St. Mary of Egypt, Liturgy of Presanctified Gifts
Week of Palms		Raising of Lazarus; Jesus' entrance into Jerusalem	

The Beginning: Forgiveness Vespers

Lent begins with Vespers on the evening of Cheesefare Sunday. Vespers is a sunset service that marks the beginning of the new liturgical day, so the observance of the first Monday of Lent begins on Sunday evening.[20] Vespers begins as usual, until the intonation of the Great Prokeimenon ("Turn not away thy face"). This same prokeimenon is appointed to Vespers on the second and fourth Sundays of Lent.

The beginning of Lent is marked by a specific moment. The vestment colors and coverings in the church are changed from gold to purple during the vesperal intonation of the prayer "Count us worthy, o Lord." The rest of the service follows the particular Lenten order for the Liturgy of the Hours and includes the first time the community prays the "Prayer of St. Ephraim the Syrian" together.

The primary feature of the beginning of Orthodox Lent is the communal exchange of forgiveness.[21] The order for this short and profound ritual varies widely among Orthodox people. The rite originated from the monastic custom of performing prostrations of humility, asking and receiving forgiveness, and exchanging the kiss of peace. There are essentially two methods for observing this inaugural Lenten rite. The maximal pattern begins with the presider kneeling before the assembly, asking for their forgiveness, and performing a prostration before everyone with the words "forgive me, a sinner." The people respond with "God forgives, as I forgive" and ask for the forgiveness of the presider. In some communities, the people form a circle so that everyone exchanges this rite with everyone else in the congregation, sealed with the kiss of peace. Meanwhile, the

20. Russo, "Origins of Lent," 180–88.

21. Denysenko, "Rituals and Prayers."

choir sings paschal hymns to capture the joy and the destiny of Lent. A number of variations of the full pattern exist, and they typically include the presider's request for forgiveness with the people's response. In some instances, the presider will exhort the people to exchange forgiveness and leave it up to them to greet those with whom they wish to perform the exchange. The source for the rite is the Gospel lesson appointed to the Cheesefare Divine Liturgy, where Jesus commands his disciples to forgive. This commandment connects the Lenten quest to commune with God with the need to reconcile with estranged people.

The Vespers of Forgiveness reveals the inner meaning of Lent. Christ's death on the cross and resurrection removes the barrier alienating humankind from God. It is not possible for any Christian to be reconciled with God without partaking in the sacrament of the brother and sister. Reconciliation is celebrated in heaven and on Earth. The path to communion with God occurs in community and in the context of the particular communal situations people engage in everyday life.

The Primary Features and Rites of Lent

In our objective to inform the reader with an emphasis on the inner meaning of the liturgical year, we will not repeat all of the precious historical information on the development of Lent in Orthodoxy. These remarks will be limited to essential information.

There is one noteworthy difference between the Sundays and weeks of Lent and the preparatory period. There is no overarching theme or scheme governing the commemorations and Gospel lessons of the Sundays of Lent. Bertonière has demonstrated that commemorations of the Lenten Sundays appeared rather late in history and came to displace a simpler rhythm of Markan lessons.[22] The Sunday of the Cross, marking the midpoint of Lent, was the only significant thematic commemoration. The other Lenten Sundays represent the monastic stewardship of the church's liturgy that began to take clear shape in the post-iconoclastic period.[23]

The commemoration of the Triumph of Orthodoxy on the first Sunday of Lent is the best evidence of this stewardship. It is a Sunday celebrating Christ's incarnation in the flesh and the legitimacy of worshiping him and

22. Bertonière, *Sundays of Lent*, 42–44.

23. Miguel Arranz argues that the church appointed the themes of these Sundays for dogmatic and pastoral purposes. See Arranz, "Les 'fêtes théologiques,'" 54–55.

venerating Mary and the saints in images.[24] The rites associated with this Sunday are quite solemn and include processions of icons and even the chilling intonation of the anathemas of heretics and schismatics in their fullest forms. This first Sunday is quite popular among the people, especially since children tend to participate in parish icon processions. There is, however, nothing particularly Lenten about this first Sunday.

The same principle holds true for the second, fourth, and fifth Sundays. Orthodoxy remembers St. Gregory Palamas on the second Sunday.[25] The hymnography appointed for this feast includes numerous anti-Latin polemic tropes along with the veneration of St. Gregory's teaching on the essence and energies of God and the people's participation in the divine life. The fourth Sunday remembers St. John Climacus (of the Ladder) and the fifth, St. Mary of Egypt. The lives of these two saints and St. John's famous writing (on the divine ascent) certainly express the ideals of a spiritual life, which include models for prayer, fasting, keeping vigil, forgiveness, repentance, and refraining from anger, among many others.[26] These themes resonate deeply with the spirit of Lent and are quite compatible with Sunday commemorations. It is essential to note, however, that these two saints exemplify the ascetical life and the monastic stewardship of the liturgy that is again responsible for their appointment to these Sundays.

The Gospels assigned to the Sundays of Lent reveal a simpler rhythm of the Word, based on a semicontinuous reading of the Gospel of Mark. When one detaches the monastic commemorative appointments to these Sundays, their themes are somewhat unremarkable, and this may seem problematic in comparison with the powerful messages of the Sundays of the preparatory period. The absence of commemorations in the older Lenten rhythm of Sunday celebrations suggests that Lenten observance was quieter and less active until the church began to add new saints and rites.

The current existence of several Lenten liturgical fixtures makes Lenten observance much more active for the faithful Christian. Most parishes celebrate the Liturgy of Presanctified Gifts (PRES) one or two times each week. In his seminal study on the history of this service, Stefanos Alexopoulos shows that the PRES originated as a service at which the people

24. See Getcha, *Typikon Decoded*, 184–86 for the historical background.

25. See the second and third troparia on ode three of the second canon at matins for examples of anti-Latin themes in *The Lenten Triodion*, 319. For a brief commentary on the gradual emergence of manuscript evidence of Lenten Sunday commemorations of these saints, see Bertonière, *Sundays of Lent*, 92–93.

26. For an English translation, see Climacus, *Ladder of Divine Ascent*.

could receive Holy Communion on non-eucharistic days.[27] PRES could even be celebrated during non-Lenten seasons. Its confinement to Lent was the result (again) of the monastic stewardship of the liturgical tradition. Currently, Orthodox Christians attend PRES on Wednesdays and/or Fridays of Lent. This permits them to receive Communion on weekdays when the Divine Liturgy is not offered. In other words, the church does not offer the Eucharist on the weekdays of Lent.[28] This is compatible with the notion of Lent as a quieter, simpler season devoted to prayer.

Another example of the tension between the quiet Lenten rhythm and liturgical busyness is the appointment of the services of St. Andrew of Crete.[29] Andrew composed this lengthy hymn for monks who were preparing to die and meet Christ, as expressed by its stark penitential character. The canon migrated to the fifth Wednesday of Lent. It was distributed in four parts, one for each of the first four days of the fifth week, because of its great length. In the Slavic tradition, the canon migrated to the first week of Lent, when it is currently read in four parts (Monday through Thursday), and then again to the fifth Wednesday of Lent. The chanting of the canon occurs with Compline, and during the fifth week it also contains the reading of the life of St. Mary of Egypt. These services of the first and fifth weeks are, again, popular; people participate in them. It is noteworthy that they did not originate as Lenten services, but migrated from their native contexts to Lent. The population of the Lenten season with extra services on weekdays resulted in the intensification of the liturgical experience for parish communities.

The fifth week of Lent features the "Akathistos Hymn" in addition to the commemoration of St. Mary of Egypt.[30] The "Akathistos Hymn" is a long poem reflecting on the mystery of the incarnation and invoking Mary, the Mother of God, to intercede on behalf of the Christian faithful. The hymn's literary style follows the pattern of the late-antique kontakion; it is a poem consisting of some twenty-four stanzas performed by a soloist. Orthodox hymnography is a primary source for theology and

27. Alexopoulos, *Presanctified Liturgy*, 8–40.

28. An exception occurs when the Annunciation falls during Lent.

29. See Getcha, *Typikon Decoded*, 173–77, for a historical survey of St. Andrew's Great Canon. See also Getcha, "Grand Canon." See the important analysis by Krueger, *Liturgical Subjects*, 130–63.

30. For a discussion of the scholarship on the authorship, date, and theology of the "Akathistos Hymn," see Pentcheva, *Icons and Power*, 12–17. See also the seminal study of Wellesz, *Akathistos Hymn*.

is essentially the main vessel for promulgating Greek patristic theology in the church's liturgy. The kontakion was the most profound theological hymn of the Orthodox repertory until it was reduced to a shortened verse that was the companion of the troparion. The "Akathistos Hymn" is the successor of the kontakion, retaining the length, complexity, and profundity of its historical antecedent.

The "Akathistos Hymn" composed in Mary's honor was written between the fifth and seventh centuries and is of unknown authorship, though it is often attributed to Romanos the Melodist (sixth century).[31] The one assigned to the Matins of the fifth Saturday of Lent was likely composed for the Annunciation, given the prominence of its incarnational tropes. The appointment of the Annunciation to March 25 (April 7, OC) resulted in its constant occurrence during Lent. It was so popular that it separated from the official liturgies of the Annunciation and became a permanent fixture of the fifth Saturday of Lent. In addition, it became a blueprint for new Akathists, and several hymns have been composed in honor of Christ and many saints, including Panteleimon, Nicholas, and Michael the Archangel.

The "Akathistos Hymn" is particularly beloved in the Greek Orthodox tradition. It is customary to sing selections from it (also known as "Salutations") each Friday evening of Lent. This practice is similar to the division of the "Canon of St. Andrew of Crete" into four parts, sung Monday through Thursday of the first or fifth weeks of Lent. The "Akathistos" is sung in its entirety on the fifth Saturday (Friday evening of the fifth week in parish practice). These services tend to be popular; they represent the continuation of strong Marian piety in the church.[32] On the fifth Saturday of Lent, the Divine Liturgy is celebrated in memory of the Mother of God, completing the weekly pattern of Marian commemoration during Lent.

The first and fifth weeks of Lent are the most liturgically active because of the "Canon of St. Andrew of Crete" and the "Akathistos Hymn." Does this mean that these weeks are the most important of Lent? The coincidence of the liturgical commemoration of St. Mary of Egypt and the Mother of God in the fifth week seems to indicate some kind of special theological feature. This liturgical intensity inspired Thomas Hopko to refer to the week as one of "the two Marys."[33] His description was partially true; in the experience

31. Jeffreys and Nelson, "Akathistos Hymn."

32. See Pentcheva's remarks on the shift in Marian piety exhibited by the "Akathistos Hymn" in Pentcheva, *Icons and Power*, 12–17.

33. Hopko, "St. Mary of Egypt."

of the people who participate in the services, the week is indeed an enco-mium to Mary, Mother of God, and Saint Mary of Egypt. History teaches us that these liturgical commemorations were not originally composed for Lent but migrated there. This does not mean that these commemorations are not suitable for Lent, as one could certainly argue that this is the result of the organic development of the liturgy. The penitential character of the "Canon of St. Andrew" and the life of St. Mary of Egypt is wholly compat-ible with Lent. It seems that it is Lenten solemnity itself that functions as a kind of magnet drawing certain liturgical practices to the season. The result is a plethora of liturgical services and an intense experience for those who attempt to observe the fullness of the season.

In summary, there are essentially two faces of Lent. One depicts a season of quiet prayer, vigil, and listening to the proclamation of the word of God. The addition of the "Prayer of St. Ephraim the Syrian" to Lenten daily practice provided the most constant rehearsal of penance, which reso-nates with the themes of humility and return from exile inaugurated in the preparatory period. The current practice of restricting the celebration of the Divine Liturgy to the Saturdays and Sundays of Lent fits the character of quiet prayer and vigil. Participants not only fast from certain foods but also gather less frequently for the offering of the liturgy. The decreased fre-quency is fitting, because it resonates with the pattern of Jesus' withdrawal into the wilderness for forty days of prayer and fasting.

The tendency to baptize catechumens at the Paschal Vigil made Lent a period of intense preparation. Egeria's description of Jerusalem's sta-tional liturgy in the fourth century establishes it as a busy liturgical season from the late-antique period.[34] We have also seen that the understanding of Lent as a holy season contributed to its tendency to act as a magnet that attracted liturgical services originally designated for non-Lenten purpos-es. These factors combined to make Lent a liturgically busier holy season than any other time of the church year. It is unlikely that the Orthodox Church would take any actions to reduce the sheer number of liturgical services, but the reality of multiple liturgical services prohibits the faithful from devoting more time to the quiet, private, and domestic observances of prayer, vigil, and almsgiving. There is simply no way to reconcile the intense busyness of Lenten liturgy with the practice of quiet prayer and vigil. The continued privileging of Lenten liturgical intensity over quiet

---

34. See Maraval, Díaz y Díaz, and Valerius, *Égérie journal.*

domestic observance makes the pastoral exhortations for the faithful to make time for the latter unrealistic.

Holy Week

Orthodox Holy Week is like Lent in the profound solemnity assigned to it. Its liturgical theology is anchored in an extensive series of scriptural lessons, especially in the seemingly constant proclamation of the Gospel. The observant Christian who hears the proclamation of the Word attentively can receive incomparable blessings.

Like Lent, however, Holy Week has become a magnet for liturgical traditions that are particularly popular among the people. Two are particularly outstanding: the communal celebration of the mystery of Holy Unction observed on Wednesday and the rituals surrounding the veneration of the epitaphios (*Plashchanitsa* in Slavonic), the embroidered burial shroud of Christ. The intensity of Lent increases by a few degrees for Holy Week.

The Intermission: Raising of Lazarus and Feast of Palms

Ironically, most Orthodox Christians do not know that Lent ends during Vespers on the Friday of the sixth week (of Palms). Holy Week begins with the Matins of Holy Monday, celebrated on Sunday night in parishes (more on this soon). Two related feasts take place in between the end of Lent and the beginning of Holy Week: the raising of Lazarus, and Palm Sunday, also known as the Entry of the Lord into Jerusalem.

Like the Sundays of the preparatory period, the Gospel reading provides the primary source for the Liturgy of Lazarus on Saturday (John 11). This popular service is observed with the Liturgy of St. Basil, and the replacement of the "Trisagion Hymn" with the baptismal variant (Gal 3:27) reveals this feast as an occasion for baptisms. In this sense, Lazarus Saturday seems to be more prominent than the Liturgy of Palm Sunday even if the latter has a higher ranking in the church's official system.

Scholars have referred to Lazarus Saturday as a key point of evidence in understanding the beginning of Lent.[35] The festal character of the day represents the end of the Lenten period and the Church's initiation of new

---

35. See Talley, *Origins of the Liturgical Year*, 181–82. Bradshaw and Johnson present the state of the scholarship in *Origins of Feasts*, 115–17.

Christians through baptism and anointing.[36] The baptism of neophytes on Lazarus Saturday may come from a period of Church history when it was necessary to distribute baptisms over a series of services to avoid overwhelming the Paschal Vigil. Despite the disappearance of mass baptisms, the day has retained its festal character simply because it marks the end of Lent and prefigures the promise of the resurrection through the raising of Lazarus. Palm Sunday is one of the highest feasts of the church, with no after-feast period. Its primary feature is inaugurating the historical commemoration of Christ's passion and resurrection. If Lazarus Saturday represents the fusion of baptism with the church's most festive seasons, Palm Sunday exemplifies liturgical mimesis. The mimesis of the events of the life of Christ in the liturgical program of Holy Week is the only reason that Palm Sunday has no after-feast, as the church moves on to the next theme.

Monday, Tuesday, Wednesday: Bridegroom Matins

Orthodoxy shares a common core with the Western churches in its rich liturgical celebration of the Paschal Triduum, beginning with the offices of Holy Thursday through Paschal Vespers on Sunday afternoon. Like other seasons, Holy Week expanded in history to include liturgical celebrations on Monday, Tuesday, and Wednesday.[37] Parishes and monasteries that fulfill the ideal pattern of liturgical celebration pray the Hours, the Liturgy of Presanctified Gifts, and the Bridegroom Matins on these days. The "Prayer of St. Ephraim the Syrian" is recited communally for the last time on Wednesday, and the appointed Gospels for Holy Week PRES are long and convey the spirit of liturgical mimesis. The extension of Lenten practices beyond the completion of Lent simply demonstrates the changing sense of when Lent ends and Holy Week and Pascha begin in the church calendar.

The Bridegroom Matins highlight the services of Monday, Tuesday, and Wednesday. These are celebrated the evening before, so the people experience this first part of Holy Week on the evenings of Sunday, Monday, and Tuesday.[38] This pattern of moving the morning services to the evening before applies to all of Holy Week up until and including the Matins of Holy Saturday. These offices tend to be popular in the most devout parish communities, which await the special music accompanying the hymns

36. Bradshaw and Johnson, *Origins of Feasts*, 85–86.

37. Getcha, *Typikon Decoded*, 211–14.

38. See Calivas, *Great Week*, 29–49.

along with the thematic Gospels. The most profound hymn is attributed to Kassia, a female hymnographer of the ninth century who was abbess of a monastery in Xerolophos in Constantinople and an opponent of iconoclasm.[39] She composed a hymn appointed to the Matins of Holy Wednesday (sung on Tuesday evening), the doxastikon of the aposticha.[40] The hymn praises the harlot who anointed Jesus' feet with myrrh and wiped them with her hair, a theological reflection on the Gospel appointed to this Matins, John 12:17–50.

Two aspects of the Holy Wednesday service and the "Hymn of Kassia" illuminate a pattern of Holy Week that begins with these Bridegroom services and continues to Pascha and beyond, through the period of Pentecost. The first is the tendency for the hymns of the service to create profiles of secondary characters who appear in the Gospel narratives. These hymns identify Judas as the primary antagonist, the villain to be avoided at all costs. They label him as a traitor and apostate. He is often compared with other secondary heroes who reveal the model faithful are to adopt. The harlot who anointed Jesus' feet is one of these unlikely heroes, as are the wise thief (from the Lukan narrative), Joseph, and Nicodemus. The hymns represent the theological tradition of paradox—notorious sinners perform righteous acts, venerating and confessing Jesus as the rightful king and God, while his own disciples abandon him, with one of them (Judas) committing the most dreadful act.

Numerous musical settings have been composed to decorate the "Hymn of Kassia." Alexander Lingas notes the popularity of this hymn in Greece, asserting that even people who don't attend church frequently will attend the Matins of Holy Wednesday just to hear it.[41] The "Hymn of Kassia," then, is one of a few examples of liturgical components that become popular among the people and are therefore important in interpreting and understanding the meaning of the season.

The Service of Holy Unction on Wednesday

The evening of Holy Wednesday has diverse liturgical celebrations within the Orthodox Church. While the churches of the Slavic tradition pray the Matins of Holy Thursday, the service of Holy Unction has become a fixture

39. See Zugravu, "Kassia the Melodist," 7.

40. For an English translation of the complete text, see *Lenten Triodion*, 540–41.

41. "Episode 7: Hymns of Kassianí."

in the Arabic and Greek traditions. The cathedral and monastic manuscripts do not mention Holy Unction as part of the Holy Week ordo, but it is important enough to be included in modern official Orthodox publications.[42] The appointment of this service to Holy Week is likely the result of the relative lack of access to confession in certain Orthodox churches. Only some priests with advanced training are permitted to hear confessions in some Greek and Arabic churches; if they do not have access to a confessor, many faithful never go to confession.[43] In its place, they could receive the sacrament of Holy Unction, as the anointing results in the forgiveness of sins.

The ascendance of Holy Unction to a permanent place in the middle of Holy Week is remarkable for many reasons. First is the separation of Holy Unction from its association with the last rites before death. Holy Unction was and remains the church's primary rite of healing and is given to all who request it. The restoration of Holy Unction as a mystery of the healing of the whole person—body and soul—was an accomplishment of the liturgical movement. Its affixation to Holy Wednesday in the Orthodox Church has made it accessible, restoring its public, ecclesial character.

There has been no widespread movement to remove Holy Unction from its celebration on Holy Wednesday. Its historical trajectory from a mystery celebrated by request to Holy Wednesday illustrates its evolution in motion and in time. One could argue that Unction's journey to Holy Week is rather new and is not supported by the manuscript tradition. This does not change the fact that many Orthodox understand Holy Unction as an essential part of Holy Week.

The Paschal Triduum

The Orthodox Triduum shares certain similarities with its Western sibling. Holy Thursday is a day for consecrating chrism and reserving the Eucharist. The Paschal Vigil was the most sacred occasion for baptizing and anointing neophytes into the church. There are also differences. Orthodox Christianity features rites of liturgical mimesis of Jesus' crucifixion and burial, while the West strips the altar bare. The West restores the singing of Alleluia to announce the resurrection, and the East replaces it with Psalm 81—the only time Alleluia gives way to a special psalm refrain in the entire liturgical year. The most significant difference between the West and the East is

---

42. See Contos, *Services for Holy Week*, 136–201.
43. See Meyendorff, *Anointing*, 56–59, and Calivas, *Great Week,* 44–46.

the West's deliberate reforms of Holy Week and Easter, especially the restoration of the Easter Vigil and the creation of the Rite of Christian Initiation of Adults. In the East, the Paschal Triduum consists of an amalgamation of traditions and services. There is a great deal of repetition of readings and hymns in the services. For the sake of brevity, we will limit the descriptions of the services to a brief summary of the historical findings and focus our presentation on problems and meaning.[44]

Monasteries and some parishes offer the complete cycle of Paschal Triduum services, listed in Table 2.3:

Table 2:3: Orthodox Paschal Triduum

Service	Day/Time of Celebration	Main Rituals/Themes	Readings
Vespers of Holy Thursday, Liturgy of St. Basil	Thursday morning[45]	Consecration of chrism, reconciliation of penitents.	Exod 19:10–19 Job 38:1–21; 42:1–5 Isa 50:4–11 1 Cor 11: 23–32 Composite Gospel[46]
Holy Friday Matins, Passion Gospels	Thursday evening	Passion and death of Jesus, cross procession.	Twelve Gospel readings
Royal Hours	Friday morning	Passion and death of Jesus.	
Vespers of Holy Friday	Friday afternoon	Unnailing of Jesus, entombment, procession with epitaphios.	Exod 33:11–23 Job 42:12–17 (LXX) Isa 52:13–54:1 1 Cor 1:18–2:2 Composite Gospel
Lamentations of Theotokos	Friday afternoon	Lamentation of Jesus' death and burial.	No readings

44. On the complex history of Holy Week in the Byzantine Rite, see Taft, "Holy Week," 155–82; Taft, "In the Bridegroom's Absence," 71–97; Getcha, *Typikon Decoded*, 211–32.

45. Some communities celebrate this service in mid-to-late afternoon.

46. Matt 26:2–20; John 13:3–17; Matt 26: 21–39; Luke 22:43–45; Matt 26:40–27:2 (see *Lenten Triodion*, 559).

Service	Day/Time of Celebration	Main Rituals/Themes	Readings
Matins of Holy Saturday	Friday evening	Lamentation of Jesus' death, harrowing of Hades, procession with epitaphios.	Ezek 37:1–14 1 Cor 5:6–8; Gal 3:13–14 Matt 27:62–66
Paschal Vigil	Saturday morning (or afternoon)	Baptism, announcement of Jesus' resurrection.	Fifteen Old Testament readings (appendix 2) Rom 6:3–11 Matt 28:1–20
Paschal Nocturne	Saturday, before midnight	Canon on harrowing of Hades and resurrection.	No readings
Paschal Matins	Sunday, midnight	Lamplighting, procession, troparion, sermon of St. John Chrysostom, paschal greetings and kiss.	Mark 16:1–8[47]
Paschal Divine Liturgy	Sunday, early morning	Divine Liturgy with paschal elements, blessing of artos.	Acts John 1:1–17[48]
Paschal Vespers	Sunday, late morning or afternoon	Paschal hymns, cross procession with Gospel readings.	

Most parish communities celebrate most of the cycle listed in Table 2.3. The services that tend to be omitted from the cycle include the Royal Hours, which repeats much of the liturgical material from the Passion Gospels, and the Lamentations of the Theotokos.[49] There is also diversity in the timing of the services. Most parishes schedule the Liturgy of Holy Thursday in the morning, but some do it in the afternoon. Some parishes move the Paschal Matins and Divine Liturgy to sunrise or later on Sunday

47. This Gospel occurs at the end of the procession at the doors of the church, before the beginning of Paschal Matins. It is proclaimed in some, not all, Orthodox traditions.

48. In some churches, it is customary to read passages from this Gospel in many languages in honor of the catholic character of the church.

49. For a description of the historical origins of the Royal Hours and its eventual acceptance in the Byzantine liturgical tradition, see Getcha, *Typicon Decoded*, 131.

morning. This diversity in the appointed times of the services does not affect the church's commitment to inverting the natural order of services by celebrating the Matins of Holy Friday and Saturday on the evenings before, while moving the Vespers of Saturday to the morning.

This situation contradicts the natural rhythm of services, and there are two issues at the center of the time change. The first is the popularity of the Matins services that feature beloved readings, hymns, and rites. The Passion Gospels and Holy Friday Matins include the singing of antiphon fifteen, "today he who hung the earth upon the waters is hung upon the cross."[50] Like the "Hymn of Kassia," this component is associated with a variety of chant and choral settings quite popular among the people. In the Greek tradition, the priest carries the cross from the sanctuary and through the church, installing it at the center and performing three prostrations while singing "We venerate Thy passion, o Christ" three times. This antiphon sets the stage for the proclamation of the sixth Gospel (Mark 15:16–32), which narrates Jesus' crucifixion for the first time in the service. This particular episode from the Holy Friday Matins is quite popular and explains in part why Matins is appointed to the evening before—so that more people will be able to attend the service without missing work or school.

The second reason some of the services are displaced from their normal appointed day and time is the sheer number of services celebrated. The existence of two rather long and somewhat complex paschal eucharistic liturgies—with the second appointed to the earliest hours of Sunday morning—necessitates bumping some of the services to earlier times to create space and attempt to prevent overburdening the clergy and choirs. The church has become accustomed to the disjointed order of services, and we will reflect on possible revisions to the schedule that would restore the services to their appointed time while permitting the people to attend them.

Holy Thursday

The Triduum begins with Vespers and the Liturgy of St. Basil on Holy Thursday, usually taken in the morning.[51] In parishes, this is a rather straightforward service. The liturgy commemorates Jesus' supper with his disciples, the events of which are narrated comprehensively by the composite Gospel

50. *Lenten Triodion*, 587.

51. For a comprehensive overview of the history of Holy Thursday, see Morozowich, "Holy Thursday."

reading. This part of the Triduum begins the liturgical mimesis of Jesus' passion and death, beginning with Judas' betrayal and the supper. This is the traditional liturgy for setting aside the reserved Communion for the sick and homebound for the entirety of the year.

Holy Thursday is much more active in some monasteries and cathedrals. Historically, penitents were reconciled to the church on Holy Thursday, received through confession and penance after their initial exile. The Orthodox Church also consecrates the chrism needed for baptismal anointings, the reception of converts, and the dedication of churches. The Orthodox rite differs from its Roman counterpart, as the consecration of chrism is an annual event in a diocesan Mass for Catholics. In Orthodoxy, chrism is consecrated on the basis of need, and the rite requires the presidency of a patriarch or other church primate.[52]

In cathedrals and monasteries, and in select parishes, it is customary to include the foot washing ceremony, with the presider washing the feet of a selection of people from the community. One could argue that Holy Thursday is the busiest liturgical day of the season, a time for ritual processes like baptism to begin (with the consecration of chrism) and end (with the restoration of penitents). It is an even older example of a magnet for liturgical customs, becoming the preferred day for annual rituals to take place. It is likely that rituals like the consecration of chrism and the restoration of penitents took place on Holy Thursday because of the conciliar nature of the eucharistic gathering, with the entire church gathered with its bishops and, in some cases, with the primate.

Matins and Passion Gospels of Holy Friday

If Holy Thursday assigns the most tasks to one ritual setting, Holy Friday has perhaps the most complex cycle of services. The Passion Gospels and Matins of Holy Friday is a lengthy service featuring twelve Gospel readings. The first (John 13:31–18:1) takes about twenty minutes. The liturgical structure itself features the proclamation of these Gospels, and they are the primary sources of the liturgical theology.

52. The ecumenical patriarch of Constantinople presides at liturgies with the consecration of chrism for many churches, including some autocephalous (independent) ones. The Russian tradition calls for the leader of each local church to preside over the consecration.

History shows some variety in the number of readings appointed to this service. Two so-called cathedral sources, the Typikon of the Anastasis (early eleventh century), and the Typikon of the Great Church (ninth through tenth century) list twelve Passion Gospels. The number of readings in Jerusalem expanded to twelve from a series of seven or eight, and it seems that the original number in the post-iconoclastic period was eleven, to match the number of the eothina resurrection readings appointed to the Matins cycle.[53] The twelfth and last reading of the Passion Gospels (Matt 27:62–66) was added to this service as a repetition of the appointed Gospel reading for the Holy Saturday Matins.

The brilliance of liturgical scholarship shows how the system of services and readings developed during a concentrated period of gradual cross-pollination between monastic and cathedral communities in Jerusalem, Palestine, and Constantinople.[54] Pott's commentary on the process, which was used to create the final list of twelve readings, is noteworthy in terms of its rationale and the mindset underpinning the enterprise. First, the compiler took four core readings from the hagiopolite witness of the fifth through the eighth centuries and came to twelve by adding seven readings from other extant Holy Friday services and the final one from Holy Saturday Matins.[55] Second, it seems that the eleven resurrection readings were the inspiration for the revision of the list from the Passion Gospels. Pott suggests that the original impetus for the revision itself was lost, and the succeeding generations could not reform the readings because of their aura of veneration.[56] Many of the readings and passages are repeated at the Royal Hours and the Vespers of Holy Friday, but it was considered improper to prune away the repetitions because of the church's veneration for the traditions themselves. It is therefore somewhat remarkable that Orthodoxy has retained the twelve readings for over one thousand years with only one published revision.[57]

---

53. Pott, *Byzantine Liturgical Reform*, 174–82.

54. See Pott, *Byzantine Liturgical Reform*, 155–73, for a lucid presentation of this enormously complex process.

55. Pott, *Byzantine Liturgical Reform*, 174–75. Here, Pott depends on Janeras's work.

56. Pott, *Byzantine Liturgical Reform*, 182.

57. The order for this service at New Skete Monastery appoints three Gospels instead of twelve and also abbreviates the number of hymns taken in between the Gospels. The editors of the order of services explain that the hymnography simply repeats what the Gospels had already proclaimed and that revision of material was necessary for clarity. See Monks of New Skete, *Passion and Resurrection*, liv–lv.

While the Gospel narratives are the primary sources of liturgical theology, people also come for other rituals. In addition to "Antiphon 15" and the placing of the cross, the exaposteilarion ("Hymn of Light") follows the eighth Gospel from Luke (Luke 23:32–49) and features numerous elaborate musical compositions. In other words, the service is a veritable festival of Scripture and hymns even if the repetition index is at a maximum.

The evangelical narration of Christ's Passion and burial continues at the service of the Royal Hours, usually on Friday morning. This service is similar to Matins, featuring several Gospel readings within the structure of the smaller hours, with special psalms appointed for thematic suitability. This service repeats much of the content from the Passion Gospels. Many parishes offer it, but it is not as well-attended or popular as the Passion Gospels.

The Vespers of Holy Friday follows the same blueprint; it is a harmony of hymnody, rite, and proclamation of the Word, as mentioned. This service has a pastoral advantage for families with scheduling conflicts to participate in the services of Holy Week. The list of appointed readings is shorter, a total of five, with three Old Testament lessons, an epistle, and another long composite Gospel. It consists of selected readings revealing the passion of Christ. Most significantly, the composite Gospel summarizes the numerous readings taken at Matins and the Royal Hours. The attentive listener hears a digest of the same message proclaimed at the earlier services.

Vespers begins a short series of two services centered on the tomb and burial shroud of Christ. On the final aposticon—another lengthy hymn set to popular musical settings—the presider and deacon incense the epitaphios, which lies on the table in the sanctuary. After the "Canticle of Symeon" and the "Trisagion Prayers," a procession begins from the sanctuary and through the interior of the church. Servers carry a processional cross, banners, and icons, while the deacon bearing incense leads the shroud-bearers, and the priest stands underneath the epitaphios, carrying the Gospel book. The procession ends with the priest placing the epitaphios on a tomb decorated with flowers. He places the Gospel on the tomb; in some traditions, the coverings used for the eucharistic gifts are placed over Christ's head and feet. This procession ends with the clergy performing three prostrations before the tomb and epitaphios and venerating the shroud with a kiss.

This first of two epitaphios processions is enormously popular among the people, who await the entire year to hear the special music composed for the processional troparion, "The Noble Joseph." The people kneel during the procession, and for many, this is the center of the service. A formidable piety of the epitaphios has developed among the people since these rites began to appear in Byzantine liturgy in the fourteenth century. In his magisterial study of the Great Entrance, Robert Taft suggests that the aer, the large veil used to cover the holy gifts at the Divine Liturgy, came to bear the image of the dead body of Christ and was interpreted as his burial shroud by select Byzantine mystagogues.[58] Taft asserts that the aer is the ancestor of the epitaphios and that the procession of the Great Entrance influenced those of Holy Week, not vice versa.[59]

The epitaphios procession remains enormously popular in contemporary Orthodoxy. People will attend these services just to see and venerate the epitaphios, as if it were a requirement for Holy Week. Once again, the appointed readings are the primary liturgical sources of Holy Friday Vespers, while popular piety elevates the ritual stature of the procession and the rites of placing the epitaphios on the tomb.

The popular Holy Saturday Matins completes the series of two services featuring the processions and rites of the epitaphios, which are more pronounced. Most of the first part of the service takes place with the clergy and people standing together before the epitaphios, holding candles. They sing the rich poetry of the lamentation hymns within the structure of Psalm 119. The service is a funeral dirge for Christ with a consistent repetition of the poles of shock and sorrow over his death and joyful anticipation of his resurrection. Furthermore, the hymnography is perhaps the most poignant living source of the theology of Christ's descent into Hades and the raising of the dead to eternal life, as expressed by these two examples: "O Life, how is it that You die? How is it that You dwell in a tomb? Yet You lay low the reign of death, and raise up the dead in Hades . . . Hades the fearsome was utterly shaken when it beheld You, immortal sun of glory, and hastily surrendered its captives."[60] The Lamentations are also set to numerous musical settings. Later in the service, at the singing of the Great Doxology, another threefold incensation of the tomb takes place, and a procession occurs with the epitaphios outdoors. In many communities, it is customary to hold the epitaphios high over the door at the entrance of the church so that the people

58. Taft, *History*, 216–17.

59. Taft, *History*, 219.

60. Contos, *Services for Holy Week*, 471, 475. It is noteworthy that the texts narrating Christ's harrowing of Hades are confined to the hymnography. There is no appointed reading from 1 Pet 3, which would provide a biblical anchor for this important theme.

walk inside underneath it while the deacon spreads incense. This is yet another poignant example of an epitaphios rite rooted in popular piety that is deeply meaningful for the people. In this case, the series of readings after the procession enhance the tensions of the two poles of sorrow and joyful anticipation. The Ezekiel pericope tells of God's promise to raise the dead by the power of the Spirit and is often proclaimed dramatically by a soloist. The composite epistle presents Paul's message on the resurrection through the leaven, while the Gospel remains focused on the sealed tomb.

Here, it is essential to remark on a significant difference between the Greek and Slavic practices of the epitaphios procession. In the Greek tradition, once the faithful have reassembled in the church, the clergy bring the epitaphios to the royal doors and then return it to its original starting point, the table in the sanctuary. The Slavs stop at the royal doors, turn around, and then place the epitaphios back on the tomb in the middle of the church. This discrepancy is important for interpreting the church's journey through the sequence of services, especially since the next service is the Paschal Vigil—a baptismal Divine Liturgy. The Greek rite essentially marks the conclusion of the period of sorrowful and joyful vigil at the tomb. The next step of the liturgical journey is to begin the series of services that celebrate resurrection. The Slavic rite keeps the focus on Christ buried in the tomb. This reveals a slight gap in the church's mindset as it navigates the liturgies of Holy Week. The Greek rite of placing the epitaphios on the table marks a turning point in the journey—it is time to transition from sorrow to joy in the resurrection. The Slavic rite does not begin the transition yet. This is a problem for one reason—keeping the epitaphios on the tomb in the middle of the church raises questions about the meaning of the Paschal Vigil, especially since it is usually celebrated on Saturday morning.

Two Paschas

We now turn to the beginning of the celebration of Pascha. Orthodoxy celebrates Pascha with multiple Eucharists drawn from the cathedral and monastic traditions. The first is the Paschal Vigil. In Jerusalem and Constantinople, photizomenoi were received through baptism at this liturgy. Baptisms are celebrated infrequently at contemporary Paschal Vigils, but the structure of the service remains essentially intact. A second set of services bears strong monastic influence and consists of Nocturne, Matins with lamplighting and procession, and a Divine Liturgy, usually just before midnight on Sunday. Both services feature dramatic rituals illustrating the final transition from sorrow to joy in Christ's resurrection.

Paschal Vigil or Holy Saturday Liturgy?

In Orthodoxy, the Paschal Vigil fits the paradigm of a service bearing hagiopolite and Constantinopolitan influences. The main components are fifteen Old Testament readings, the intonation of Psalm 81 as the prokeimenon of the Gospel instead of Alleluia, the changing of vestment colors from dark to bright, the throwing of rose petals (during Psalm 81), and the first announcement of the resurrection in the Gospel (Matt 28:1–20).[61] The Exodus and Daniel Old Testament readings are performed dramatically, with refrains chanted in each. Psalm 81 dates from as early as the ninth century (Constantinople) and early eleventh century (Jerusalem). The Matthean resurrection Gospel appears in the Armenian and Georgian lectionaries representing fifth-to-eighth-century hagiopolite liturgy.

Historically, this service was both baptismal and resurrectional. The Typikon of the Great Church states that the patriarch baptizes neophytes in the baptistery of the church during the readings. Eight readings were appointed in Constantinople. The patriarch baptized during the first seven, and they skipped the next seven and read from Daniel unless the patriarch needed more time. So, the second set of seven readings was designed for the purpose of giving the patriarch and his assistants enough time to finish the baptisms.

When the neophytes arrived, they heard the prokeimenon, the baptismal epistle (Rom 6:3–11), and joined the assembly to hear the proclamation of the resurrection in Psalm 81 and the Matthean resurrection Gospel. This service took place on Saturday evening, after Vespers. It was a Sunday service in liturgical time, which means that Holy Saturday itself was the only non-eucharistic Saturday of the year. This does not mean that this was the only paschal Eucharist—the Typikon of the Great Church calls for a Eucharistic Liturgy to take place on Sunday morning as well.

The experience of the Paschal Vigil in Orthodoxy is similar to the early twentieth-century counterpart in the West. Some parishes observe the Paschal Vigil in its fullness—including all fifteen Old Testament readings—and

61. For a detailed analysis, see Denysenko, "Psalm 81." See also the studies by Bertonière, *Historical Development,* and Arranz, "Le sacrements." Calivas comments on the displacement of the ancient Paschal Vigil in *Great Week and Pascha*, 107–8.

it is popular for families who cannot attend the midnight services. Elsewhere, it is abbreviated, with three or even fewer readings and few people in church. There is confusion on the paschal character of this service. The current rules call for a fast until the completion of the Midnight Liturgy. They presume that the faithful will remain in the church and have a snack of figs and bread to sustain them through the evening.

Pott's study addresses this "intermezzo" and identifies the central problem of making sense of the meaning of the Paschal Vigil.[62] Has Holy Week concluded and Pascha begun? Or has the Paschal Vigil become the Liturgy of Holy Saturday, the final step in anticipating Pascha, which only arrives at midnight? The inconsistency in monastic fasting practices between the two paschal services reveals some confusion on the meaning of the Paschal Vigil. The pure amalgamation of services caused this confusion, especially since the midnight services were so popular. That said, it is clear that the Paschal Vigil retained its purely paschal character by breaking the eucharistic fast and announcing the evangelical message that Christ is risen for the first time.

An unofficial tradition has emerged referring to the Paschal Vigil as the "first anastasi" (first resurrection), the initial liturgical gathering celebrating Christ's resurrection. This designation is more faithful to the historical legacy of the Paschal Vigil than relegating it to a lesser anticipatory Eucharist of Holy Saturday. Admittedly, however, this does not resolve the problem of uneven observances of this office throughout Orthodoxy.

---

62. Pott, *Byzantine Liturgical Reform*, 190–93.

The Midnight Nocturne, Matins, Liturgy

There is no doubt that the midnight offices representing the monastic tradition are preeminent in contemporary Orthodox culture even if it is, in reality, the "second anastasi." There is no denying the drama of a darkened church with the chanting of the canon, the joyful ritual of distributing the candlelight for the procession, exchanging the paschal kiss and the first greetings of "Christ is risen," "Indeed, he is Risen," the constant singing of the troparion, and the incomparable moment of standing to hear the ancient sermon of St. John Chrysostom—a rare but profound instance of a patristic reading retained in the received liturgical tradition, a true mark of paschal solemnity. The multiple dramatic liturgical rituals function as the magnets drawing people to this service. Pastors complain that people leave after the drama of the midnight procession and the initial singing of the troparion or come only for the blessing of baskets containing the traditional foods of the feast.

It is likely that the euphoria experienced at the midnight paschal services has resulted in the emergence of a series of strong liturgical moments that elevate the stature of those services and turn them into an end instead of a means. The sermon of St. John Chrysostom is a good example. One of the most frequently quoted passages from this sermon comes at the end, when he invites those who did not keep the fast or joined only at the eleventh hour to participate in the feast without hesitation or fame.[63] This passage suggests that the time for breaking the fast has arrived only then, at the series of midnight services.

It is also essential to note that the paschal services include a rare intersection of the domestic with the ecclesial and also comprise playful traditions. The blessing of paschal baskets containing the savory and sweet foods and beverages from which people abstained during the fast is a central component of the services among Slavs. No less important is the Greek tradition of marking the moment with a feast of *margheritsa*. Distributing boiled eggs to the people at the end of the service is a practice belonging to all Orthodox. Sometimes these traditions become playful, as when people engage in egg-cracking contests—an Orthodox variant of the thanksgiving turkey wishbone—or, more recently, with the tossing of eggs into a crowd of people who clamor to catch them as if they were wedding bouquets. This playfulness reveals an important layer of paschal meaning—that all has been made well in Christ's resurrection. In reality, the ministers and people can often be found smiling, laughing, and dismissing ritual mistakes with no anxiety. Pascha delivers a kind of liberation to the people, an experience of release from the tension of anticipation and the Lenten habit of daily asceticism.

The paschal midnight services mark a moment of arrival and completion. Feasting has replaced fasting, and the people exult in the good news that Christ is risen from the dead. One cannot exhaust the rich sources expressing the meaning of these services. It is essential to note, however,

63. There are numerous translations of the sermon on Pascha attributed to St. John Chrysostom published on the internet. Here is one English translation: https://www.oca.org/fs/sermons/the-paschal-sermon.

that the strong moments mentioned here tend to overshadow aspects of the paschal service that continue to exist in the church's liturgical structures but are largely forgotten in the euphoria of the moment.

The first problem is that the exhausting experience of Pascha feels like the end of the journey when it is, in fact, the beginning of a new season: Pentecost. Pascha is the first of fifty days of this joyful season. The appointed Gospel reading for Pascha (John 1:1–17) inaugurates a series of lessons that communicates the purpose of the services. The journey to and through Pascha involves encountering the living God in the flesh. The midnight service assigns the prologue of John's Gospel instead of one of the post-resurrection appearances of Christ. Those Gospels take place during the cross procession that is usually done at Paschal Vespers and are repeated throughout the liturgical year within the framework of the eleven eothina resurrection Gospels proclaimed at all Sunday Matins resurrection services.

The following section analyzes the Gospels assigned from Pascha up until Pentecost as the primary sources of liturgical theology for this period. This analysis focuses on the Sundays of Pascha up through the sixth Sunday (the Blind Man). Table 2.4 includes the Gospel for the seventh Sunday (the commemoration of the fathers of the first ecumenical council), and this is listed for context.

Table 2.4: Sundays of Pascha and Gospels

Sunday	Title	Gospel
First Sunday	Pascha	John 1:1–17
Second Sunday	Antipascha, St. Thomas Sunday	John 20:19–31
Third Sunday	Myrrh-bearing Women, Joseph and Nicodemus	Mark 15:43–16:8
Fourth Sunday	The Paralytic	John 1:1–15
Midfeast	Midfeast of Pentecost	John 7:14–30
Fifth Sunday	The Samaritan Woman	John 4:5–42
Sixth Sunday	The Blind Man	John 9:1–38
Seventh Sunday	Fathers of the First Ecumenical Council in Nicaea	John 17:1–13

The paschal Johannine pericope shifts the foundation of the festal liturgical theology from historical mimesis to a theology of revelation. These two elements remain in place during the post-paschal period and essentially alternate. The paschal Gospel reveals Christ as the true God and the only begotten son of the Father, both God and human, with whom the assembly—including the neophytes—share communion. This Gospel establishes a general pattern for the remaining period of rejoicing during the Sundays and weeks of Pascha up until Pentecost. The pattern is one of revelation, of using the Gospels as the primary sources for deepening the knowledge of Jesus for the faithful.

During this period, the church continues to sing the hymns of Pascha for the divine services.[64] The Gospel readings emphasize revelation. Those appointed to the first two Sundays after Pascha present the Johannine post-resurrection of Jesus to his disciples, including Thomas, and the visit of the Myrrh-Bearing Women to the empty tomb in Mark. The Johannine reading for the second Sunday is also the sixth eothina reading for Sunday Matins. The Markan reading for the third Sunday begins in chapter 15 to include Joseph and Nicodemus taking Jesus' body and burying it, along with the Myrrh-Bearing Women. Both readings return to the events of the resurrection by presenting the disciples' response to encountering their risen Lord and the empty tomb. They are designed to inspire reflection on the Christian core of doubt. The Christian must trust both the proclaimed word (Mark) and the appearance of Jesus (John). No other form of verification or corroboration is needed for faith. The Gospels confirm that Christians confess faith in the risen Lord, and this faith is handed on through the proclamation of the word.

The next three Sundays consist of Johannine Gospels, a selective reading of the Paralytic (fourth), the Samaritan Woman (fifth), and the Blind Man (sixth). Jesus' encounter with the Paralytic occurs near the pool in Bethesda, and his encounter with the Samaritan Woman occurs in Sychar, at Jacob's well. The encounter with the Blind Man occurs outside of the temple area. The three Gospels have strong baptismal themes. The Paralytic sought healing from the pool at Bethesda. The Samaritan Woman encounters Jesus at the well. Jesus opens the eyes of the Blind Man in an act of self-revelation, proclaiming himself to be the light of the world. The three encounters reveal the transformative healing of the people Jesus meets. Jesus heals the Paralytic and exhorts him to stop sinning. He exposes the Samaritan Woman's numerous husbands, teaches the Samaritans, and they respond with confessions of faith. After Jesus restores sight to the Blind Man, he confesses Jesus to be the Messiah and worships him.

The Gospel readings of the first six Sundays of Pascha are intentionally baptismal to deepen the communion with Christ. The resurrection Gospels address the human element of doubt, and the baptismal Gospels invite the

---

64. For an overview of the historical origins and liturgical structures of these commemorations, see Getcha, *Typicon Decoded*, 239–75.

faithful to deepen their communion with Christ through examples of his healing encounters with people in various aspects of life.

The season of the weeks and Sundays of Pascha that lead up to the feast of Pentecost feature a rich appointment of Sunday Gospel lessons and themes. This season of selective readings is similar to the Lenten preparatory period in its content, delivering a formidable collection of messages with the capacity to invite the Christian community into a more profound experience of communion with God. This season is also remarkable because of its rather abrupt move away from a precise liturgical historical mimesis. The themes are appointed to the Sundays for formative purposes. The concept of liturgical time for this season is not mimetic, but this changes with the final portion of the season with the feasts of Ascension and Pentecost.

Ascension, Pentecost, and the Meaning of Time

The penultimate section of this chapter brings us to the feasts of Ascension and Pentecost. Ascension was commemorated as part of the season of Pentecost in Christianity until it detached and became its own feast in the fourth century.[65] Pentecost originated as a Christian observance of the Jewish Feast of Weeks and became a fifty-day period of paschal rejoicing by the end of the second century.[66] Egeria describes the celebration of Ascension and Pentecost on the fiftieth day in Jerusalem in her diaries.[67]

Pentecost itself refers to both the season of fifty days of rejoicing and the fiftieth day itself. This explains the significance of the Midfeast. The aforementioned Midfeast of Pentecost refers to the midpoint of the fifty days of rejoicing from Pascha to Pentecost Sunday and not the midpoint of Pascha to Ascension.[68] The fifty-day season of Pentecost commemorated the entire mystery of salvation, including the Ascension, and was not strictly mimetic until the Ascension and Pentecost were separated in the fifth century. Furthermore, the Pentecost season celebrated the new age of God's reign inaugurated by Christ's resurrection and the Spirit's descent on the apostles. In other words, the season itself marked a significant Christian concept of time where the future of God's reign unites with the present.

---

65. Bradshaw and Johnson, *Origins of Feasts*, 69–70.

66. Bradshaw and Johnson, *Origins of Feasts*, 69–70.

67. Adam, *Liturgical Year*, 88–89; Bobrinskoy, "Ascension and Liturgy," 12–13.

68. For an overview of the liturgical history of the Midfeast, see Getcha, *Typicon Decoded*, 253–57.

The paschal cycle itself concludes on the Wednesday of the sixth week of Pascha, the day before the Ascension. This day is the leave-taking of Pascha and the rubrics call for the complete paschal character of the celebration of the services. Liturgical time transitions with the short observance of the Ascension, returning again to a precise liturgical observation of historical mimesis. The liturgical observance of Ascension is brief because of its occurrence in between the weeks of Pascha and Pentecost. The Sunday after Ascension retains the hymns assigned to the feast and features the commemoration of the fathers of the first ecumenical council in Nicea.[69] The church's prioritization of the Nicene council over the Ascension is another instance of assigning a theme important in later church history to a Sunday without a specific commemoration.

If the Pentecost season celebrates the entire mystery of salvation, Pentecost itself marks the fiftieth day when the apostles assembled and received the Holy Spirit (Acts 2). The fiftieth day refers to the experience of divine eternity in the present, the eighth day following the seven weeks of seven days. The outpouring of the Spirit on Pentecost was baptismal, so the church celebrated baptism and anointing in conjunction with this feast, followed by a one-week release from fasting requirements.

The Nicene council prohibited kneeling from Pascha until Pentecost in honor of the presence of Christ for the fifty-day season of rejoicing.[70] The practice of kneeling is restored on Pentecost with a series of prayers appointed to Vespers on Sunday evening, often celebrated after the festal liturgy on Sunday in parish practice. The Byzantine Church recites four sophisticated kneeling prayers interpolated in Vespers. These prayers are likely of fourth- or fifth-century Palestinian provenance and can be found in Constantinopolitan cathedral manuscripts of the eleventh century.[71] The contemporary text of the prayers is essentially identical to the eleventh-century Constantinopolitan texts.[72]

The first prayer addresses the Father and appears to be patterned after an anaphora. The next three prayers are all addressed to Christ. They belong to a structure that begins with the diaconal call to prayer, "Again and

69. According to Arranz, at least one manuscript appointed this Sunday to a commemoration of the first six ecumenical councils. See Arranz, "Les 'fêtes théologiques,'" 48–49.

70. Tanner, *Decrees of the Ecumenical Councils*, 16.

71. Arranz, "Les prières de la gonyklisia," 93–97.

72. Arranz, "Les prières de la gonyklisia," 97.

again, bending the knees, let us pray to the Lord."[73] The prayers themselves are predominantly penitential, asking God to forgive sins and deliver the faithful from temptation and sin. They also contain several anamnetic sections recalling Christ's descent into Hades and expressing a profound faith in the resurrection and salvation of those who have fallen asleep in the Lord.[74] Acknowledging the multivalence of these sophisticated prayers, we highlight two features. First, the kneeling prayers place repentance at the center of Christian life. The Christian who has witnessed the resurrection of Christ and heard the proclamation of the word on the Sundays of Pascha has encountered images of figures who encountered the living God and were liberated from their sin. In the kneeling prayers, the participant embraces repentance in gesture (kneeling), along with the confession of sin and a petition for forgiveness.

The second feature is the strong emphasis on the fruits of the resurrection. The primary icon of Pascha depicts Christ's descent into Hades, raising up Adam and Eve. The kneeling prayers contain multiple references to Christ's descent, and the third prayer is an elongated anamnesis of Christ's triumph followed by a petition for the salvation of the dead.[75] This prayer confirms the strong connection between Pentecost and Pascha, reiterating that Pentecost completes the joyous celebration inaugurated on Pascha. It is a festal confession of faith in the resurrection of the dead and the life of the age to come.

Pentecost originated as a season of joy in the presence of the risen Lord and is therefore Christocentric in its native form. The transition to precise liturgical mimesis narrowed the focus on Pentecost as a feast of the Holy Spirit. The feast came to bear many titles in the Eastern liturgical tradition, including "Pentecost" in the Typikon of the Great Church, but also "Trinity" (Троица) in other liturgical sources.

Ascension, Pentecost, and the Fifty Days: A Brief Analysis

The addition of new titles to the feast illustrates the influence of doctrine on its interpretation in the liturgical year. One form of the season of Pentecost

73. See *Pentecostarion*, 247–51.

74. "For, O Lord, there is no death to Thy servants, when we have departed from the body and come to Thee, O God, but rather a translation from the things that cause sorrow unto things better and more delightful, and unto repose and joy," (*Pentecostarion*, 250).

75. *Pentecostarion*, 249.

reveals a Christian concept of time that connects divine eternity with the present. In this model, Pentecost is a season of fifty days of rejoicing in the presence of the risen Lord. The joy of presence is incompatible with fasting and kneeling. It is festive and entails frequent celebrations of the Eucharist and baptisms. The season is also thematically multivalent; it encompasses the entire mystery of salvation fulfilled in Christ and is irreducible to one single event. The joy of the risen Christ brings divine eternity into the present, experienced by the faithful and neophytes with special intensity.

When the Ascension arrives in this model of Christian time, the future of divine eternity does not disappear. It is not merely a matter of Christ becoming absent after a period of intense presence and communion. Christ's ascension to heaven is necessary as the fulfillment of the promise given to all humankind: Christ's followers will participate in his Pascha, will be glorified, and will dwell in communion with God and the Spirit. The Ascension reveals Christ's seating at the Father's right hand, in the fullness of the humanity Christ shares with all.

The commemoration of Christ's ascension is also connected to the present celebration of the Eucharistic Liturgy. The church remembers the ascension of Christ and his session at the right hand of the Father in the anamnesis of the paschal mystery during the anaphora. The Ascension reveals Christ's continued exercise of the ministry of high priesthood in heaven, for the life of the church and the world.

Boris Bobrinskoy connects the commemoration of Christ's ascension with the Pentecost that occurs at each Eucharistic Liturgy. Bobrinskoy demonstrates that as the body of Christ and with Christ as its head and high priest, the church invokes God to accept the eucharistic offering and send the Holy Spirit upon the gifts and the faithful during Christ's session at God's right hand.[76] Bobrinskoy's analysis of the inseparable connection between Christ's ascension to heaven and Pentecost evokes the spirit of Pentecost as a season of rejoicing and receiving the gift of the Holy Spirit because Christ enables his body, the faithful of the church, to petition God at the heavenly altar.

When Christians observe Pentecost in the second, related model—the commemoration of the fiftieth day—the outpouring of the Spirit celebrates and sustains communion with the glorified Christ and his Father. Christ is not absent, but the emphasis of the church changes—it is oriented toward the completion of the journey, so the remainder of

---

76. Bobrinskoy, "Ascension and Liturgy," 20.

life in the world points towards the final entrance into divine eternity. Divine eternity is outside of time and is neither subject to decay nor the limitations of the created world. Eternity is therefore not confined to the heavenly realm; divine grace permits the church to enter into eternity and to allow it, along with the kingdom of God, to shape the church's experience and mission in the present world.

This analysis of Ascension and Pentecost emphasizes the meaning of the paschal mystery in Christ's continued ministry of high priesthood in his session at God's right hand. When the church gathers for liturgy, it joins Christ in petitioning for God's grace and mercy and, therefore, participates in the life of God outside of time. The theological emphasis is on the relationship between God and the church, which involves petitioning, offering, and receiving. The gift of citizenship in God's kingdom for eternity underscores this emphasis. It may seem, then, that the strong trinitarian themes are undervalued in this analysis. Christ's ascension, his session at God's right hand (with the church), and the sending of the Spirit upon the church is thoroughly trinitarian. There is simply no need to add a new title to the feast (such as Trinity to Pentecost) and transform it into a *doctrinal* solemnity, because the entire celebration of the liturgical year is trinitarian by nature.

In summary, then, the Ascension and Pentecost establish the rhythm of liturgical prayer for the bulk of the year. The purpose of these feasts is to continue to deepen communion with Christ, the risen Lord and God of the Christian people.

The Sundays after Pentecost: Orthodox Ordinary Time?

The paschal-Pentecost cycle governs much of the liturgical year outside of the fixed feasts. What, then, is the significance of the part of the liturgical year that does not feature the themes of the paschal mystery or other major festal cycles? The week after Pentecost is a festal octave—Monday commemorates the Holy Spirit, and the first Sunday of Pentecost is Sunday of All Saints.[77] It has become customary for some local churches to celebrate their particular synaxis of saints on the second Sunday after Pentecost. The fourth Sunday is devoted to the memory of the fathers of the first six ecumenical councils. The twelfth remembers the fathers of the seventh ecumenical council. The

---

77. *Pentecostarion*, 264–81. A more detailed analysis of the Sunday of All Saints occurs in chapter 4 of the present study.

pattern of assigning commemorations of major events in church history to select Sundays appears again here and demonstrates the significance of the first seven ecumenical councils in Orthodox liturgy.

Readings are appointed for thirty-two Sundays after Pentecost, and adjustments are made to the readings, depending on the calculation of Pascha and the beginning of the preparatory period. Most of the Sundays in the first part of the series of thirty-two follow a semicontinuous reading from Matthew. The twentieth through twenty-sixth Sundays coincide with Advent. Most of the Sunday Gospels are Lukan, with specific pericopes assigned to the Sundays before and after the feasts of Christmas and the Theophany.

The governing principle of the Sundays after Pentecost—which constitute much of the liturgical year—is Sunday. With the exception of the conciliar commemorations, Orthodoxy practices a semicontinuous reading from Matthew and Luke for this portion of the liturgical year. The Johannine readings are reserved for the Sundays and weeks of Pascha, and most of Mark is assigned to weekdays. Two parts of this cycle of Sundays after Pentecost are adjusted to prepare for the cycles of the incarnational and paschal seasons. This means that the theme driving the meaning of these Sundays of Pentecost is the primordial feast of Sunday itself.[78] These Sundays retain the original meaning of resurrection, and while the Octoechos provides the material reflecting on the resurrection in repeated cycles of eight, it is the cycle of eleven resurrection Gospels appointed to Matins, and not liturgy, that defines the meaning of each week.

Furthermore, each Sunday is a celebration of the paschal mystery. The themes explored throughout this chapter appear in the prayers, especially the anaphoras of the Orthodox liturgy. Schmemann consistently identified the Divine Liturgy as an act of the assembly's ascension to the kingdom of God. This ascension connects the assembly to Christ, who intercedes for the church and world in his session at God's right hand. God sends the Spirit to the assembly to receive the gifts they have presented. Every Sunday, then, is a commemoration of the Ascension and Pentecost and ushers the faithful into the unending day of the kingdom, as described by Alkiviadis Calivas.[79] One might think of Sunday as the

78. For an overview of the history of Sunday in early Christianity, and the scholarly debate on the similarities and differences between Sunday and the Sabbath, see Bradshaw and Johnson, *Origins of Feasts*, 3–28. See also the study of Rordorf, *Sunday*; Searle, "Sunday"; and Pope John Paul II's 1998 Apostolic Letter *Dies Domini*.

79. Calivas, *Liturgy in Dialogue*, 215.

ordinary celebration of the paschal mystery, with the annual calendrical commemoration being extraordinary.

Conclusions

This chapter has reviewed the movable cycle of the Orthodox liturgical year by presenting a digest of the historical development of the key elements and focusing on the meaning of the seasons and their central celebrations. We conclude with brief reflections on the following observations. The movable cycle developed historically as an expansion of a smaller, original collection of commemorations. This expansion has resulted in liturgical repetitions and a vast amount of content assigned to the services. The second issue concerns the relationship between the preparatory period and the Lenten cycle of services, given the profundity of the themes appointed to the Sundays before Lent. We then conclude with the potential of the Sundays of Pascha and the Ascension-Pentecost cycle.

The movable cycle in Orthodoxy has historically been liturgically intense. Jerusalem's Liturgy testifies to daily services that increase in intensity through Pascha, a phenomenon that remained remarkably constant in the holy city's liturgical sources despite the destruction wrought by Persian and Arab invasions. Constantinople also had its own intense liturgical cycle in the Liturgy of the Great Church, which set the pattern for the surrounding parishes. The current Orthodox liturgies of the movable cycle are the products of a series of exchanges between the cathedral and monastic traditions and reworkings of the orders for cycles and specific offices. The scholarship of Janeras, Taft, Pott, and Galadza presents multiple examples of communities that revise their native traditions by incorporating elements from a neighboring cathedral or monastic practice. The readings and hymns appointed to the services of Holy Week are among the clearest examples of this phenomenon.

It is not unusual for liturgies to accumulate content from diverse sources over the centuries. The question posed to the contemporary church is whether or not it can or should sustain a tradition that has accumulated content with no attempt to prune the services. The churches of the West have periodically revised their services by excising certain elements, while the Orthodox Church has resisted appeals for change. Most of the discussion has centered on the philosophy of liturgical development, as a certain school of thought views revision as a violation of the organic progression of liturgy. The other school of thought tends to view revision as necessary.

Perhaps a middle ground could be identified for the current Orthodox system: modest pruning to make the services more manageable for parish clergy and singers. The analogy is that of a tree: it is necessary to trim the branches occasionally to keep the tree healthy. An honest assessment of parish human resources—clergy and singers—is necessary to ascertain how much parishes can and cannot handle. Parishes with numerous full-time clergy and singers are rare. The standard community has one priest and music leader and is fortunate to have one deacon.

Certainly, some Orthodox communities revise the order of services to make them manageable. These revisions are unofficial, local emendations that are neither recorded nor codified in the official service books. The Monks of New Skete exercised their monastic autonomy in creating a new order of services that draws from tradition. The logical next step for Orthodoxy is to create a new blueprint or pattern for a parish Holy Week. The pattern would be adjustable on the basis of parish human resources. The Passion Gospels and the Matins of Holy Friday are a good example. One pattern might call for the twelve Gospels with only one hymn accompanying each. Another model might restore the Paschal Vigil to the evening of Holy Saturday and move the traditional Matins and Divine Liturgy to the following morning (instead of midnight). Some scholars have called for the creation of an Orthodox catechumenate culminating with the restoration of baptism during the Paschal Vigil. This is a noble idea worthy of further discussion, with the understanding that such celebrations might need to take place in designated places with the staff capacity to manage the services (such as diocesan cathedrals or an annual parish rotation in a deanery).

The primary point from this investigation is to acknowledge that the current movable cycle is an amalgamation of services containing content from numerous historical sources. The original native communities of these services had the staff to execute the offices. One simply cannot assume that each parish is able to sustain the model of a movable cycle that continues to bear the legacy of community conditions no longer in existence.

The second issue is the tendency for new liturgies to grow and expand outside of the original core. The preparatory period for Lent is the best example of this growth. The Constantinopolitan core featured two preparatory Sundays with the themes of gradual immersion into fasting, judgment, and forgiveness. Over time, this cycle was expanded to feature humility and reconciliation. The preparatory period now consists of four Sundays, or even five, if one includes Zacchaeus and/or the Canaanite Woman. It has become nearly as long as Lent itself.

The Sundays of the preparatory period are more Lenten than the current commemorations of Lenten Sundays. Throughout this chapter, we observed the tendency of the church to remember the most important events of its history on precious Sundays. These include the Triumph of Orthodoxy and St. Gregory Palamas on the first two Sundays of Lent, along with a series of fathers of the ecumenical councils distributed throughout the movable cycle. The connection of the themes for the Sundays of Lent to Lent itself is weak, even for the fourth and fifth Sundays (of St. John Climacus and St. Mary of Egypt). We have also identified the fifth week of Lent as an instance of intense devotion, with the "Canon of St. Andrew," the Vita of St. Mary of Egypt, and the "Akathistos Hymn."

These developments leave us with two outcomes. The first is a long preparatory period of Sundays that are thoroughly Lenten, and the second is the perception that Lent requires more frequent and intense liturgical participation. Alexopoulos's research on PRES reminds us that the original purpose of this service was to sustain the people with Holy Communion when they were not celebrating Divine Liturgy. Celebrating the Eucharist less frequently is a way of observing the spirit of the fast, as the time is devoted to prayer, vigil, fasting, and almsgiving performed on one's own, quietly and privately. This rhythm of Lent collides with the current tendency to schedule multiple services each week, often accompanied by public lectures, meals, retreats, and gatherings.

Could the church once again alter its observance of Lent? One possible revision would be to retain the earlier stratum of two preparatory Sundays (Meatfare and Cheesefare), while moving the Publican and Pharisee and Prodigal Son commemorations to Lent.[80] The appointment of these Gospels to Lent, along with the introduction of the "Hymn of Repentance" and Psalm 137, would enrich the Sunday worship experience. The second revision is to restore Lent as a season of quiet prayer that does not require attendance at multiple liturgical offices. The Presanctified Liturgy would remain in place as the office for receiving Communion in the absence of a weekday liturgy. This revision would require a significant adjustment in pastoral ministry to promote Lent as a season devoted to quiet private observance as opposed to increasing attendance in communal assemblies.

80. Moving Zacchaeus and the Canaanite Woman to Lent is also a possibility.

The Sundays of Pascha and the Ascension-Pentecost cycle are similar to the preparatory period in the profundity of the themes assigned to them. The reality for Orthodox communities is that all of the energy is invested into exhorting people to attend Lent and Holy Week services. The people are exhausted after concluding the marathon of the Holy Week cycle, and the richness of the Sundays of Pascha is muted as people rest from the liturgical intensity of the previous period.

The readings and themes of the Sundays of Pascha depict a season of rejoicing in the presence of the risen Lord. This season is designed to strengthen faith and deepen communion in Christ. The historical development of liturgy alternates between those that celebrate the entire mystery of Christ and those that tend to set aside days for historical mimesis. Most of the Pentecost season retains a sense of celebrating the fullness of Christ's incarnation and resurrection—the appointment of the Ascension to the fortieth day and the remembrance of Pentecost as a trinitarian feast narrow the Church's focus to doctrinal precision.

The Pentecost season never lost the capacity for mystagogical formation for both the faithful as well as for neophytes. It is a time for all to experience the gift of citizenship in God's kingdom anew and to be reminded that the future—divine eternity—shapes the present as much as the past. A quieter Lenten observance and a more manageable Holy Week could contribute to the restoration of the season of Pentecost as one of profound spiritual renewal. The annual commemoration of the feasts of this long season can also enhance the experience of ordinary time as equally transformative, since the church participates in Christ's session at God's right hand and receives the gift of the Spirit each and every Sunday it gathers for Divine Liturgy.

3

The Fixed Cycle

C HRISTIANS MEMORIZE SPECIFIC DATES on the liturgical calendar. These dates belong to the fixed cycle of feasts and commemorations that take place on the same date every year. The fixed cycle has several smaller families in the Orthodox liturgical year. The largest is the incarnation cycle, consisting primarily of Christmas, Theophany, and Hypapante (Meeting), along with secondary and tertiary commemorations.

Marian feasts form a large family, especially the four main observances of Mary's birth, entrance into the temple, annunciation, and dormition (assumption). A series of feasts of St. John the Baptist surround his birth, beheading, and the three findings of his head. The final family is the sanctoral cycle, remembering saints, which includes hundreds of feasts. The sanctoral cycle is one of the oldest and provided a blueprint for Marian feasts. Two feasts of the Lord do not fit neatly into any of these families but are prominent in the Orthodox tradition: the Transfiguration of Christ and the Exaltation of the Holy Cross.

The historical development of the fixed cycle of feasts is complex, and this chapter analyzes a selection of the festal families. We begin by surveying the primary cycle of incarnational feasts and examine Theophany and the eventual appearance of Christmas as a sibling. Multiple factors contributed to the calculation of the dates for feasts, including the ebbs and flows of agricultural patterns and the marking of seasons on the basis of solar position. The main aspects of historical development include the significance of the *dies natalis* (birthday) and its conversion into the anniversary of the death of a loved one as a feast.

Our primary thesis on the fixed cycle is twofold. The fixed cycle of feasts has powerful paschal overtones and essentially distributes a series of paschal celebrations associated with events in the lives of Christ and Mary (in particular) throughout the liturgical year on fixed dates. The paschal themes are especially salient in the Theophany and Dormition feasts, so most of the discussion will focus on those interconnections.

The second thesis concerns local community memory as the primary factor that shaped and continues to form the fixed cycle. Essentially, a core community associated with a particular place gathers on an anniversary of a beloved figure's death to celebrate the person. In Orthodox Christianity, such gatherings generated a wide variety of narratives and liturgical practices associated with significant places and objects of the person's life. Feasts commemorating wonder-working icons and epic events in the history of nations will be presented and analyzed in the chapter on everything else. This chapter will narrow its focus to the primary feasts of Christ and the high-ranking feasts of Mary and John the Baptist.

This chapter does not follow the traditional order of the Orthodox calendar. The Orthodox liturgical year begins on September 1, the Indiction feast and the beginning of the year for the Roman Empire. Byzantine lectionaries follow this traditional order, and the current scheme of feasts has a logical structure. The first major feast following the Indiction is Mary's Birth on September 8, and the last major feast is her death on August 15. In other words, the liturgical year begins and ends with the beginning and ending of *Mary's* earthly life. The structure of the liturgical year is also innately paschal. The second major feast occurs only two weeks after Indiction, and it happens to be the Exaltation of the Holy Cross (September 14). This book attempts to articulate the meaning of the liturgical year and therefore delivers a presentation of the main cycles instead of a precise chronological description.

Feasts of the Incarnation

In the Orthodox tradition, three great feasts constitute the core of the incarnation cycle: Christmas (December 25), Theophany (January 6), and Hypapante (Meeting, February 2). Christmas and Theophany have preparatory periods with a strict fast day preceding each and a forty-day fast in advance of Christmas.

A number of secondary feasts take place after the primary observances. December 26 is devoted to the synaxis of Mary, and December 27 is the feast of Stephen the Protomartyr. The church celebrates the circumcision of

Christ on January 1, an instance of historical mimesis in the liturgy. January 7 marks the synaxis of St. John the Baptist, and February 3 celebrates the memory of St. Symeon and the Prophetess Anna. Hypapante takes place forty days after Christmas—more historical mimesis in the liturgy. Numerous cultural rituals of fasting, feasting, and music have developed within this festal season, and these contribute to the cycle's meaning even if they are not officially inscribed in the liturgy.

Christmas

The earliest lectionary evidence of the Church of Jerusalem testifies to a celebration of the incarnation on January 6, followed by the fortieth-day commemoration on February 14.[1] A separate celebration of Christmas occurred in Antioch as early as the fourth century, and the Emperor Justinian imposed the Constantinopolitan system of three incarnational feasts—Christmas, Theophany, and Meeting—in Jerusalem in the sixth century.[2]

Much of the scholarship on Christmas concerns the theories on the history of the calculation of the date for the feast. Two competing hypotheses on the selection of December 25 emerged in the liturgical academy of the twentieth century and dominated the discussion.[3] The first is the history of religions hypothesis. This scheme suggests that the legalization of Christianity in the early fourth century caused a natural gravitation of Christmas to the pagan winter solstice feast, resulting in the appointment of Christmas to December 25. The second theory suggests that the Annunciation was the first incarnational feast and led naturally to calculating Christ's birth on December 25—precisely nine months following his conception in Mary's womb. No consensus has emerged among scholars on the hypotheses, but the two schools share one common element: the tendency for significant feasts to gravitate to seasonal solar markers.

---

1. See Getcha, *Typicon Decoded*, 126–27.

2. For an informative discussion on the historical influence of Constantinople on Jerusalem in this instance, see Galadza, *Liturgy and Byzantinization*, 239–40.

3. Roll, *Origins of Christmas*.

Essential Elements of Christmas

Orthodox Christmas has a short preparatory season, especially the Sundays before Christmas and the short period of the pre-feast.[4] The season begins forty days before the feast, with a seasonal fast that always begins on November 15. The length of the fast demonstrates both the high rank of the season and Great Lent as its blueprint. The season of the Christmas fast, however, is not as intense as Great Lent, since there are major differences in the content and order of the services. The fast is titled St. Philip's Fast (its first day), and the season has the unofficial title of Advent, though it is quite different from its Western sibling.[5] Hints of the coming festal celebration begin after November 21, the Entrance of the Theotokos into the Temple. The *heirmoi* of the canon of Christmas are added to the Matins services after this date, the primary festal preview until the Sunday before Christmas.[6]

There are two preparatory Sundays with similar themes. The Sunday of the Holy Ancestors of God commemorates the patriarchs Abraham, Isaac, and Jacob, and the Church observes the Sunday of the Holy Fathers in the next week. The Sunday before Christmas is the main day of preparation, remembering the three patriarchs again. The Gospel reading of the Matthean genealogy presents the main theme (Matt 1:1–25). It includes the announcement of the birth of Christ, which seems designed to confirm Jesus as the fulfillment of God's promise, the legitimate heir of the patriarchs and kings, linked to Abraham and David in the text.

The Greek Orthodox tradition has retained the Constantinopolitan practice of commemorating the prophet Daniel and the three holy youths on the Sunday before Christmas. Their feast day is December 17, but their inclusion in the Christmas preparatory period is both incarnational and paschal. The episode of God sparing the youths from annihilation in Nebuchadnezzar's furnace reveals Christ as the fourth in the furnace with them in Daniel 3. The furnace itself has strikingly paschal overtones, especially

4. For a detailed description of the daily liturgical offices, see Getcha, *Typicon Decoded*, 129–31.

5. The Christmas Fast begins on the day after the commemoration of St. Philip. See *Typikon*, 269–72. Lev Gillet makes an intriguing distinction between the Western and Eastern themes of the incarnation. He depicts the West as awaiting the coming of a liberator and placing a stronger emphasis on Christmas. Gillet says that the East's primary theme is light overcoming the darkness with the Epiphany as the heart of the three feasts. See A Monk of the Eastern Church, *Year of Grace*, 46.

6. The *heirmos* is the first song in a series of short, poetic hymns constituting a canon. The *heirmos* expresses the theme of the biblical canticle underpinning the canon.

since this lesson is the final Old Testament reading of the Paschal Vigil, proclaimed even if the patriarch has completed baptisms. The liturgical structures of the two preparatory Sundays, then, is theologically determinative on the basis of the Gospels and appointed themes.

The preparatory period for Christmas increases in intensity December 20 through 24, with numerous hymns and lessons appointed to the services that reflect the Orthodox theological reflection on the incarnation.[7] Historically and in the present, the most intense day is Christmas Eve. This day retains a strict fast, a vestige of an earlier stratum of a shorter preparatory period. It is an especially busy liturgical day, complete with numerous lessons appointed to the Royal Hours, Vespers followed by the Liturgy of St. Basil, the Vigil consisting of Great Compline and Matins, all completed by the Divine Liturgy of Chrysostom on the morning of the feast. The system of Christmas services is somewhat complex, and special rubrics guide pastors on the order to be followed, depending on which day of the week Christmas falls. Table 3.1 presents the order of services, depending on the day of the feast.

Table 3.1: Order of Services for Christmas Eve and Morning

Christmas on Tuesday, Wednesday, Thursday, Friday, and Saturday.	Christmas on Sunday and Monday
Royal Hours	Royal Hours (prayed on Friday)
Vespers	Liturgy of St. Chrysostom
Liturgy of St. Basil	Vespers
Great Compline	Great Compline
Matins	Matins
Liturgy of Chrysostom (Christmas morning)	Liturgy of Basil (Christmas morning)

The reshuffling of services for Christmas on Sunday and Monday represents the retention of the main order of services for Sunday. The traditional vigil of Vespers and Matins on Saturday evening remains intact without the Compline office. This order also removes eucharistic services from Saturday or Sunday evenings. In other words, the order and rhythm of the Sunday

7. See, for example, the exapostilarion (hymn of light) of the forefeast, which explains Christ's coming as a paradox—the one who dwells in an unapproachable light is born of a virgin, in *Festal Menaion*, 216.

synaxis itself remains generally intact with only a few additions. This exception is important, as it is a reminder of the solemnity of Sunday as the primary weekly synaxis. The revision is also confusing for pastors, however, because it requires adjustment to the usual order of Christmas services.

The received tradition represents the later monastic retooling of a somewhat simpler order of services observed in the Greek cathedral tradition. The basic principle for the cathedral rhythm of Christmas services was multiple Eucharists, two Divine Liturgies celebrated within a twenty-four-hour period. When the Church celebrates a feast with two Eucharists, it expresses the high rank of its solemnity. The Theophany order of services (for the eve and day of the feast) is exactly the same as Christmas. This designation shows that Christmas and Theophany join Pascha as the most solemn feasts of the year, superior to all others. Table 3.2 presents the order of services for Christmas in the Typikon of the Great Church.

Table 3.2: Order of Christmas Services for the Typikon of the Great Church

Christmas Eve	Christmas Day
Matins	Matins
Vespers with seven Old Testament readings	Divine Liturgy
Divine Liturgy	
Vigil	

Clearly, the Constantinopolitan cathedral celebration of Christmas was quite full, featuring two solemn Divine Liturgies, one on the eve and the other on Christmas morning.

The Liturgical Theology of Christmas: Gospel and Hymnography

The schedule of readings and selection of hymns assigned to Christmas provides us with the liturgical theology of the feast. Table 3.3 lists the readings assigned to the two primary liturgies and the vigil.

Table 3.3: Select Readings for Christmas Liturgical Offices

Office	Readings
(24 Dec) Vespers	Gen 1:1–13
	Num 24:2–3, 5–9, 17–18
	Mic 4:6, 7, 5:2–4
	[responsorial psalmody]
	Isa 11:1–10
	Bar 3:35–4:4
	Dan 2:31–36, 44–45
	[responsorial psalmody]
	Isa 9:6–7
	Isa 7:10–16; 8:1–4, 9–10
(24 Dec) Liturgy	Heb 1:1–12
	Luke 2:1–20
(25 Dec) Matins	Matt 1:18–25
(25 Dec) Liturgy	Matt 2:1–12

The gospel readings appointed to the primary services of Christmas are taken from Luke and Matthew. There is no deviation from historical mimesis to make theological statements, as in the Roman rite. The richest set of readings is the one appointed to the Vespers and Liturgy of Christmas Eve. The order of lessons draws deeply from the prophets and presents Christ as the fulfillment of the promise God made to Israel and Judah. God will act to establish his kingdom of righteousness among his people. The selection of readings connects Jesus to the line of David, coming from Bethlehem Ephrathah. In other words, the kingdom of God has come into the present from the future through the birth of Jesus.

The message of the presence of the kingdom and the urgency of pursuing it is coupled with the strong soteriological themes in the hymns. The first sticheron on Psalm 140 at Vespers uses paschal language to speak of the salvation given to God's people through Christ's birth. The hymn (attributed to Germanos) announces the reopening of paradise to humankind and claims that the cherubim guarding the entrance to paradise with a flaming sword is no longer there.[8] This is the same kind of language used to describe Christ's salvation of humankind on the Sunday of the Cross during Lent.[9]

The hymns emphasize the divine condescension; Christmas is not a celebration of a "new Cyrus" but a call to worship God, who has come to be the people's righteous king. They are filled with doxological exhortations, including the reference to Christ as the image of the Father in the first hymn and the numerous descriptions of God as "pre-eternal."[10] These exhortations are certainly compatible with the Christmas narrative of the magi, who recognize Christ as God and worship him. The hymns repeat an exhortation: come and worship him.

Contemporary Problems with Pastoral Liturgy and a Christmas Suggestion

The problem confronting much of the Orthodox world on Christmas is attendance, especially in places where Orthodoxy is a minority among other Christian churches and religious communities. For Orthodox churches that have adopted the revised Julian calendar, Christmas falls on the same day and time as the Western Christian celebration. Many Orthodox people make compromises with families and are unable to attend the entire cycle of services. Furthermore, in Western culture, it is quite normal for families to attend services on Christmas Eve and to devote mornings to domestic duties. The result is that many families find themselves at the vigil service of Great Compline and Matins. To be sure, this service features excellent hymnography, but it has only one lesson from Scripture (Matt 1:18–25), which happens to be the Matthean report on the birth of Christ proclaimed as part of the genealogy on the previous Sunday.

Acknowledging that rigorists would encourage people to attend the entire cycle of services, the Christmas cycle is structured to provide a convenient solution for both families and pastors of smaller communities. The Vespers and Divine Liturgy is rich in both Scripture—with eight Old Testament readings—and hymnography. This service retains the unique structure of cathedral worship with responsorial psalmody intercalated in between Old Testament lessons.[11] The service invites the

---

8. *Festal Menaion*, 253.

9. See *Lenten Triodion*, 342–43.

10. See the festal kontakion in *Festal Menaion*, 261.

11. See Mateos, *La celebration*, 17–18.

people's participation, a highly desirable feature of any solemn liturgical office, especially Christmas. Finally, the service invites the people to hear the Lukan version of the narrative of Christ's birth.

It is pastorally advantageous to move the Vespers with liturgy to later in the day to allow people to partake of the most scripturally rich eucharistic celebration of the feast. While attendees will miss the liturgy on the following morning, they will still have participated fully in the festal liturgical ordo through the reception of Holy Communion. For smaller communities that are unable to observe the complete order of the cycle, the Vesperal Liturgy could function as the primary service of the cycle. The unitive nature of the cycle itself makes this pastoral adjustment possible. The Gospel readings appointed to the services are not anticipatory but announce the birth of Christ. The offices are not a progression in time that leads to a finale on Christmas morning but instead provide a number of opportunities for the people to observe the solemn feast.

The Theophany Feast: Overview and Meaning

The Theophany on January 6 is anchored in the Christian liturgical tradition. Multiple late-antique Christian voices attest to its centrality, including St. John Chrysostom, who testified to the blessing of waters on this feast.[12] Its earlier title in the manuscript tradition was "Feast of Lights," a name that endured into the ninth and tenth centuries until it was eventually supplanted by Theophany.

The Armenian tradition continues to observe Theophany as an incarnation feast that is not limited to the event of Jesus receiving baptism from John in the Jordan. We discussed the theme of paradox in Christmas, the divine condescension, with the creator assuming the flesh and human life of creation. Theologians reflecting on the Theophany expand the same theme of paradox of the creator receiving baptism—for the forgiveness of sins—from the hand of one of his creatures.

Theophany may be the center of the triad of three incarnational feasts, and not only because it is the second of the three. It features the most unique liturgical office, the blessing of the waters. It also has poignant paschal tropes distributed throughout its hymnography.

---

12. See Chrysostom, *De Baptismo Christi,* 365–66.

The Structure of Theophany Services

The preparatory period of Theophany is similar to that of Christmas. It begins with the Sunday before Theophany, which reads from the beginning of the Gospel of Mark (1:1–8). The structure for Theophany Eve is the same as Christmas, including the Royal Hours, Vespers with the Liturgy of St. Basil, Vigil (Great Compline and Matins), and Divine Liturgy on the day of the feast. Theophany also includes the complex office for the blessing of waters. This service usually takes place on the day of the feast, after liturgy, though it is customary to have two blessings, one indoors and one outside.[13]

Some Byzantine manuscripts also appointed the blessing of waters to the Vigil.[14] At the Great Church of Constantinople, the water blessing occurred after the main liturgy, in the church, followed by another water blessing in the courtyard that employed a separate prayer. Like Pascha and Christmas, Theophany is a unitive feast. It begins with the first office of the cycle and culminates with the Eucharistic Liturgy. The water blessing typically occurs only once, so this feature distinguishes Theophany from the other feasts with multiple Eucharistic Liturgies.

Table 3.4: Theophany Readings[15]

Theophany Service	Appointed Readings
Saturday before Theophany	1 Tim 3:14–4:5; Matt 3:1–11
Sunday before Theophany	2 Tim 4:5–8; Mark 1:1–8

13. For a brief consideration of pastoral options on the timing for the water blessing, see Denysenko, *Blessing of Waters and Epiphany*, 176–78.

14. Denysenko, *Blessing of Waters and Epiphany*, 177.

15. For details, see *Festal Menaion*, 314–87.

Theophany Service	Appointed Readings
Vespers and Divine Liturgy	Gen 1:1–13
	Exod 14:15–18, 21–23, 37–29
	Exod 15:22–27, 16:1
	Josh 3:7, 8, 15–17
	2 Kgs 2:6–14
	2 Kgs 5:9–14
	Isa 1:16–20
	Gen 32:1–10
	Exod 2:5–10
	Judg 6:36–40
	1 Kgs 18:30–39
	2 Kgs 2:19–22
	Isa 49: 8–15
	1 Cor 9:19–27
	Luke 3:1–18
(6 Jan) Matins	Mark 1:9–11
(6 Jan) Liturgy	Titus 2:11–14, 3:4–7
	Matt 3:13–17
Blessing of Waters	Isa 35:1–10
	Isa 55:1–13
	Isa 12:3–6
	1 Cor 10:1–4
	Mark 1:9–11

The Vespers of Theophany has thirteen readings, drawing abundantly from the Pentateuch to demonstrate God's salvation of his chosen people through the instrumentality of water. The readings present instances of theophanies through water. These include the ark of the covenant at the Jordan in Joshua, the dew that appeared on Gideon's fleece, God's appearance at the altar in the confrontation with the servants of Baal and Elijah (1 Kgs), and God's deliverance of Israel from captivity in the Exodus account. The epistle readings contain references to the appearance of God, and the entire cycle refers to the synoptic accounts of Jesus' baptism in the Jordan by the hands of John. The predominant themes, then, are theophanies and covenant, the return to God and the divine law.

The Blessing of Waters—Annual Renewal of Baptism

The rite of the blessing of waters is a unique feature of the Theophany feast and a ritual highlight of the entire incarnational cycle. The primary prayer of the rite ("Great Are You") probably originated as an Antiochene-type anaphora, a text that was edited for the blessing of waters. There is evidence suggesting that multiple editors revised baptismal variants of "Great Are You."[16] The history of the rite testifies to additional prayers, including one over the water for healing, along with diverse gestures of sanctification. In the current rite, the priest immerses a cross into the water as the primary gesture of consecration. The history of the rite testifies to other gestures, such as the pouring of chrism (Armenian) and the placement of fiery charcoals (Maronite).[17]

16. Denysenko, *Blessing of Waters*, 83–102.
17. Denysenko, *Blessing of Waters*, 68.

For Theophany, the blessing of waters functions as the most pro-found source of liturgical theology. The aforementioned readings—espe-cially those appointed to the Vespers with liturgy—are prominent in the liturgical components of the blessing of waters. This is particularly true of the text of the prologue and an anamnetic portion of the "Great Are You" prayer. These texts refer to God's saving activity in Exodus, 1 Kings, and at the Jordan. The liturgical texts develop a sacred topography surrounding the Jordan, as Jesus' entrance into the waters is an instance of God appearing again, now as in the past.

When parishes assemble to celebrate the blessing of waters, they receive the gifts granted by God to the chosen people in the past. The epiclesis of the prayer expresses the blessings granted to participants, including healing, protection from evil, and remission of sins. The texts represent the Church's imagination on the profundity of the divine act. A troparion of the Great Church in Constantinople claims that Christ's entrance into the Jordan transformed it into a furnace that purged the sins of all those who entered.[18] The manuscript tradition contains numerous texts of the prologue of the blessing of waters. One of those texts claims that those who partake of the water are experiencing deification, the process of partaking of the life of God and becoming like him.[19]

The blessing of waters is enormously popular among Orthodox people, and it always has been. A pilgrim to sixth-century Jerusalem reported the excitement of Alexandrians who dove into the water from their boats as soon as the rite was completed.[20] People are attuned to the healing properties of the waters. They bring empty jars to the service and fill them, using the water for healing the soul and body when they become ill. They drink the water and anoint themselves with it, and the presider sprinkles them when he blesses the church toward the end of the rite. In warm climates, the presider attaches the cross to a rope and tosses it into a public body of water. A type of competition takes place among young people, who race to fetch the cross. In cold climates, the people carve large crosses at the location for the blessing of waters. It is now customary for people to jump into the frigid waters at the conclusion of the blessing in a type of Orthodox polar plunge. While many of these activities are on the periphery of the rite, they express the people's desire to deepen their communion with God by entering the water. In the consciousness of the church, Christ has entered the water again, "now as then," during the rite.[21]

18. A hymn from *Codex Paris Greek 1590*, a twelfth-century manuscript representing Constantinopolitan liturgy, states that the Jordan became a furnace through Christ's descent and removed the sins of those baptized there. See Denysenko, *Blessing of Waters*, 162.

19. A verse from the prologue in *Codex Athens National Library 663* (14–15 cc.) states that the faithful are in the process of deification, in Denysenko, *Blessing of Waters*, 132n28.

20. Antoninus, *Antonini Placentini Itinerarium*, 135.

21. The epiclesis of the rite invokes Christ to be present "now as then" through the

The blessing of waters brings the sacred topography of the Jordan into each parish and body of water where communities gather for the rite. The ritual acts of blessing, sprinkling, anointing, and partaking of the waters renew the baptismal covenant with the living God. The entire feast itself is a reflection on the mystery of the divine condescension. The one who was born of a virgin and deigned to assume human nature receives baptism for the forgiveness of sins at the hands of his creation.

The multiple allusions to the Markan account of Jesus' baptism are important here. Jesus' first appearance is at the Jordan to receive baptism and to be led by the Spirit into the wilderness for fasting. The blessing of waters invites his disciples to receive these baptismal blessings and to follow him, with him leading the way, "now as then."

Descent into Jordan, Descent into Hades

Theophany is a feast celebrating Christ's victory over Hades. In this sense, it is thoroughly baptismal, since the rite of baptism itself is one of casting out demons, ending the covenant with the Evil One and devoting oneself entirely to Christ. The blessing of baptismal waters contains numerous rites and references to casting out demons from the waters, a theme that the Theophany water blessing retains.[22]

The Theophany water blessing refers to Christ's victory over death and Hades as well. The verses of the prologue in the manuscript tradition again provide suitable examples, such as this verse: "Today the abyss is sunk in the pool from the one who comes down, and the creator of all is baptized in the water."[23] Evil cannot withstand the creator of all—demons who serve the Evil One must obey his command and depart from the space he enters, a space designated for those who will enter into covenant with him.

A verse from another Byzantine liturgical manuscript makes a bolder claim about the significance of Christ's baptism in the Jordan: "Today the death of disobedience occurs in the Jordan river, and the sharpness of wandering and the union of Hades is destroyed in it; our Lord and God Jesus Christ releases sin and grants a baptism of repentance to the world." Jesus

---

power of the Holy Spirit. See *Festal Menaion*, 357.

22. These themes are more prominent in the baptismal blessing of waters and are retained by the Theophany rite. See Denysenko, "Baptismal Themes."

23. A verse from the prologue in the tenth-century Euchologion *Grottaferrata GB VII*, cited from Denysenko, *Blessing of Waters*, 109.

destroys Hades upon entering the Jordan—his baptism releases humankind from captivity to sin and to death. This is a central aspect of the paschal character of baptism—by partaking in Christ's death and resurrection, neophytes receive renewed human nature and crucify sin. The verses of the Orthodox liturgical tradition that explicitly connect the Theophany event to Pascha are significant, representing Theophany as a paschal feast.

The depiction of Christ's descent into the Jordan as a journey to Hades to recover Adam, who is lost, is an ancient theological idea rooted in Syriac literature, particularly in the *Homily on Epiphany* of Jacob of Serug (521 CE).[24] Jacob sets the stage for Jesus' baptism in the Jordan by depicting a dialogue between Jesus and John the Baptist in which John does not understand the purpose of Jesus' baptism, since he is fully divine and sinless.[25] Jesus explains that he descends into the water to recover Adam so that the image that has become faded might be cleansed, an image of the universal cleansing of humanity through Jesus' baptism.[26] Sebastian Brock and Kilian McDonnell both point out that Jacob is simply sustaining a theological theme already established in the Syrian tradition by Ephrem, though his soteriological claim is clearly linked to Jesus' baptism in the Jordan.[27]

The position of the Theophany feast on the liturgical calendar creates challenges for facilitating full participation. For those on the revised Julian calendar, it takes place a few days after the turn of the New Year and coincides with the end of family travels and the resumption of school. Many people are unable to attend a weekday service. Some parishes have moved elements of the Theophany feast to the following Sunday, especially the blessings of waters.

The Theophany is unitive like Christmas—it is not a progression of services, inching through time to arrive at the finale remembering Jesus'

24. See Jacob of Sarug, *Jacob of Sarug's Homily*; Brock, "Baptismal Themes," 236–39; and McDonnell, *Baptism of Jesus*, 156–67.

25. Jacob of Serug, *Homily*, nos. 181–201 (26–30).

26. "Our Lord says 'I am not lacking but in one thing: the recovery of Adam who was lost from me is being sought by me. Allow me to descend to seek Adam, the fair image, and when I find him the whole of my desire shall be fulfilled. It became a great search for me in his case and on account of that I have come, and it would be a deficiency if I cannot find the lost one. The recovery of him, that alone is what is lacking with me: to regain Adam who was willing to perish at the hands of the evil one. In this recovery my desire will come to perfection, because Adam is needed by me to enter into his inheritance. Therefore, allow me to descend to cleanse the image that has become faded, lest it too would remain deficient, should you withhold me,'" (Jacob of Serug, *Homily*, nos. 201–12 [36]).

27. Brock, "Baptismal Themes," 326–29; McDonnell, *Baptism of Jesus*, 162–67.

baptism on January 6, but the observance begins with the first service. Like Christmas, those who participate in the Vespers and liturgy receive the blessing of a tapestry of Scripture on God's coming and salvation of his chosen people. For communities that want to maximize the people's participation, it might be wise to move the water blessing to the following Sunday to include those who cannot attend during the week because of work and school obligations.

Hypapante (Meeting) as the Completion of the Incarnation Cycle

The third feast of the incarnational cycle is the Hypapante (meeting or encounter), an ancient feast bearing many titles throughout tradition. This feast commemorates the Lukan account of the elder Symeon and prophetess Anna meeting the infant Jesus and rejoicing at his coming. The feast would appear to be one of mere mimesis, and in Orthodox culture, it tends to be regarded as lower in ranking. One reason for this is that some Orthodox regard Hypapante as a Marian feast, even though it has the highest rank in the Orthodox festal system.[28] Western influence on Orthodox thought is likely to have influenced this Marian categorization.

In its earliest hagiopolite form, Hypapante was a great feast. Egeria described its solemnity, as did Hesychius of Jerusalem (fifth century), who referred to it as the "feast of feasts."[29] Egeria referred to it as the fortieth day after Epiphany, whereas the fifth-century Armenian lectionary identifies it as the fortieth day after the Nativity (Christmas).[30] It is possible that the title was slowly becoming standardized as Hypapante by the fifth century, since both Hesychius and the Georgian Lectionary use this title. The Georgian Lectionary appoints an Old Testament reading (Isa 19:1–4) expressing an eschatological theme to the liturgy, along with the standard Lukan account. The notion of meeting was not only one of Symeon's historical encounter with Christ, but the preparation of the faithful to meet him in his second coming.

28. See *Typikon*, 471.

29. See Maraval, Díaz y Díaz, and Valerius, *Égérie journal de voyage*, 254–57 (*Egeria* hereafter). See also Aubineau, *Les homélies festales*, 1–5.

30. See Renoux, *Le codex arménien*, 229; *Egeria*, 254–55.

The contemporary celebration of the Hypapante in the Slavic tradition resembles a Marian feast.[31] The rubrics call for blue vestments, and there are no festal antiphons for the Divine Liturgy. The Hypapante does not observe the two Eucharist pattern characteristic of Pascha, Christmas, and Theophany. It has three Old Testament readings appointed to the Vigil, standard for feasts of its rank. There is one anomaly: it has its own introit, a feature of the feasts of Christ, despite the absence of festal antiphons (among the Slavs).[32]

The Hypapante feast concludes with a blessing of candles, which are then distributed to the faithful. Processions of clergy and faithful took place on the occasion of Hypapante in Rome, Jerusalem, and Constantinople. The procession in Jerusalem was similar to other processions, such as the one on Palm Sunday. The people were participating in a rite to meet the Lord, possibly going southwards from Jerusalem to Bethlehem.[33] Certainly, one can interpret this rite as liturgical mimesis in its hagiopolite context. The sacred topography of liturgy in Jerusalem is a significant factor here. The standardization of this practice in the contemporary Orthodox rite has both mimetic and eschatological overtones. The Incarnation feasts present Christ as God who assumes flesh to the faithful. They meet him as a newborn child (Christmas), an adolescent (Hypapante), and an adult (Theophany). They use candles to light their way to meet him at his second coming.

31. The appointed station for this feast is the Blachernai Church devoted to Mary in Constantinople, which may be one reason why some Orthodox view the feast as Marian (see Mateos, *Typicon*, 220–25).

32. *Festal Menaion*, 431.

33. Groen, "Festival of the Presentation."

The Incarnational Cycle: Summary Observations

This chapter confirms what is obvious to devout Christians: the feasts of the incarnational cycle are among the most solemn of the liturgical year. The inner meaning of this festal cycle is less obvious. Its observance is a manner of participating in paschal feasts of the Lord appointed at annual times of the liturgical year. The sheer duration of the cycle in the received tradition is weighty. Among the diverse rhythms of the liturgical year, it is the most similar to the paschal cycle because of its forty-day preparatory period and its length of forty days.

There are numerous reasons the incarnational cycle came to be so elaborate in the life of the church. Two tendencies in the development of liturgy converged to elongate and complicate it. The first was the tendency for the church to commemorate feasts of the Lord on the basis of historical mimesis, although we concede that the method for calculating the date of Christmas falls outside of this possibility.

There is logic to this pattern even if we temporarily remove Christmas from the equation. Egeria identifies the solemnities of the Epiphany during her fourth-century travels, and what we now know as the Hypapante feast was celebrated with fanfare forty days after the Epiphany.[34] The Armenian Lectionary appointed Hypapante to February 14, further evidence of a feast

---

34. *Egeria*, 250–57.

uniting Christ's birth with his baptism. Christmas eventually becomes a separate fixture on the liturgical calendar, and a number of lesser feasts emerge through the course of time. The synaxes of Mary on December 26, John the Baptist on January 7, and Symeon and Anna on February 3 exemplify the pattern of new commemorations appearing alongside major ones—instances of the expansion of a festal period.

The second pattern is the one of a solemn season as opposed to a short but intense one-day commemoration of the feast. The strict fast appointed to the eves of Christmas and Theophany might evince an older stratum of the pattern of fasting and feasting for a major holiday. The forty-day fast and forty days of commemorating the incarnation resemble Lent and the significant post-paschal period of fifty days of rejoicing (or forty if one counts only to the ascension). Liturgical seasons grow and become more complex unless they are pruned. Therefore, the expansion of these feasts throughout history should not be surprising.

The growth of the incarnational cycle and its expansion into a series of greater and lesser festal commemorations imparts a crucial lesson. These feasts have been unitive, celebrated over the course of two days with two liturgies (for Christmas and Theophany). The richness of the Old Testament lessons assigned to Vespers beckons the people to see that the God who saved his chosen people in the past has come and is coming again to save them in the present. They are then invited to follow him into the water, which he makes into the saving spring of the Jordan, bringing the sacred topography of the past to each assembly of the present. They are assured that touching the water by sprinkling, anointing, and drinking is participation in death and resurrection. He forgives their sins and renews their nature after his image, delivering them from captivity to death, as he released those who had been bound in Hades. The Hypapante feast invites them to prepare to meet him yet again—a reminder that the Christian life is a journey. The reality of paschal themes saturating the entirety of the incarnational cycle, and of the faithful who experience this Pascha in their lives, supersedes an analysis of the number and types of liturgies assigned to this season.

The incarnational cycle confirms the hypothesis on the liturgical meanings of time and place. The appointment of these feasts to annual dates on the calendar and the multiple references to divine activity in the past illuminates the past-present dynamic prevalent in Christian liturgy. The phrase from the water blessing epiclesis—"now as then"—is an instance of this dynamic. Nevertheless, the liturgies show that the present-future dynamic is equally salient. The Theophany is particularly demonstrative in this regard—partaking of the holy water now continues the process of transformation that equips the participant for their future life with God. The people's yearning to be with God in the present, exemplified through the festive fasting of Holy Supper and the desire to touch God in the consecrated water, reveals the inner desire to belong to the community of God. This raw yearning is in no way reducible to restoring the past. The sacred topography of the rites observes a similar principle. The faithful participant does not need to make a pilgrimage to the Jordan to encounter the living God. God comes to each assembly, no matter where they are gathered, and makes their water into the Jordan. This is possible only through the power and love of a God who is not subject to the laws of time and can make himself everywhere present, filling all things.

The Marian Cycle of Feasts

Orthodoxy is like the Roman Church in its observance of a rich Marian festal cycle. Four feasts constitute the primary core of this cycle, and a number of smaller feasts accompany them. Mary's Birth (September 8), Entrance into the Temple (November 21), Annunciation (March 25), and Dormition (August 15) are the four chief feasts. The vast majority of this section's analysis engages the four central Marian feasts. Numerous feasts of Mary concern her relics, such as her belt and icons painted in her honor. Some of these liturgical days will be discussed in the chapter on everything else.

The Marian cycle began to take shape in the milieu of the Council of Ephesus (431) after Mary received the title of Theotokos. The pattern of festal development follows that of both Christ and the saints, as some Marian commemorations are associated with sacred topography—particularly the Dormition. Marian feasts introduce two new elements to this study of the liturgical year. First, they represent the significance of tradition in shaping Christian rite and prayer, especially since three of the four central feasts are not recorded in the New Testament. These represent a different element of historical mimesis. The second aspect is the meaning of feasts that commemorate the life of someone other than Christ and how they straddle the line dividing worship and veneration. The development of Christian doctrine and Mary's identity as the mediator between

God and humanity exercised significant influence in the population of Marian feasts on the liturgical calendar.

Mary's Birth (September 8)

The Marian cycle begins with her birth on September 8.[35] The cycle of services reveals a pattern for much of the Marian cycle. Table 3.5 presents the core readings appointed to most of the great Marian feasts:

Table 3.5: Composite Table of Readings for Great Marian Feasts

Birth, Dormition	Entrance[36]	Annunciation[37]
	Vespers	
Gen 28:10–17	Exod 40:1–5, 9, 10, 16, 34, 35	Gen 28:10–17
Ezek 43:27—44:4	1 Kgs 7:51; 8:1, 3–7, 9–11	Ezek 43:27—44:4
Prov 9:1–11	Ezek 43:27—44:4	Prov 9:1–11
		Exod 3:1–8
		Prov 8:22–30
	Matins	
Luke 1:39–49, 56		
	Liturgy	
Phil 2:5–11	Heb 9:1–7	Heb 2:11–18
Luke 10:38–42; 11: 27, 28	Luke 10:38–42; 11: 27, 28	Luke 1:24–38

The composite chart shows remarkable consistency for the readings appointed to Matins and Liturgy. The Annunciation is the only exception for the Gospel readings, for obvious reasons. This is the one feast where there is some semblance of historical mimesis. There is much more variation in the Old Testament and Epistle readings. The Genesis, Ezekiel, and Proverbs readings are assigned to most of the feasts and constitute a kind of core for

35. See *Festal Menaion*, 98–130.

36. *Festal Menaion*, 164–98.

37. *Festal Menaion*, 435–67.

many Marian commemorations. These readings represent Marian typologies dating from early Christianity. Mary is a ladder into heaven (Jacob), the closed gate in Ezekiel (representing her virginity), and the epitome of wisdom (Proverbs 9). Mary is often compared with Eve in the feasts, as Christ is to Adam. The wisdom reading underscores Mary's obedience to the divine law, a central theme appearing in all of the feasts.

The Old Testament readings appointed to the Entrance and Annunciation expand the Marian typologies. The Entrance readings present God's command to Moses to construct the ark of the covenant, the vessel bearing the divine law of the Ten Commandments and God's presence. The reading from 1 Kings recalls Solomon's construction of the temple and the place designated for the ark. These readings combine to present Mary as the ark and temple, the one who bears God's presence.

The Annunciation Old Testament readings from Exodus and Proverbs are theophanies. The Exodus reading is another expansion of Mary as the God-bearer, the bush bearing the eternal fire. The Proverbs pericope prefigures Christ as the eternal God, and the inclusion of this reading manifests the deeper meaning of the word Theotokos: Mary will give birth to the eternal God.

The Gospels for these feasts are all taken from Luke. The Matins Gospel is the same for all four feasts, presenting Mary's encounter with Elizabeth, the response of John to Mary's news from Elizabeth's womb, and Elizabeth's famous acclamation: blessed are you among women, and blessed is the fruit of your womb. The Annunciation Gospel pericope presents Gabriel's visit to Mary, his announcement of the conception of Jesus, and concludes with Mary's acceptance of the news. The Gospel for the other three central feasts is from Luke 10/11, featuring two instances of Jesus emphasizing the priority of hearing God's word, along with the acclamation of the blessing of Mary and her womb from an anonymous woman in the crowd. The Gospel presents Mary as the model for Christians to follow for hearing God's word.

Marian Feasts: Historical and Christological

The Marian feasts represent an important turning point in the development of the liturgical year. In some respects, they continue to follow the patterns observed in the feasts of Christ. For example, the Annunciation is a central event of the New Testament and salvation history and belongs to the model of historical mimesis, at least in part. The Dormition involves sacred topography because of the legends of the apostles gathering at Gethsemane for Mary's death and passage into heaven. In this sense, the earlier development of the cult of the saints contributed to the Dormition, along with the theology of saints as intercessors for the church. The two specific new developments associated with the core Marian feasts are the promotion of Mary as central character in Christology and the rapidly evolving sense of her as the primary mediator for the church and humankind. These are the primary themes expressed by the hymns appointed to the feasts.

Mary's title of Theotokos is christological. The conciliar definition safeguards Christ's divine nature. The core Marian feasts are inherently christological even if they appear to feature specific events in Mary's life. Mary's birth, entrance, and Dormition do not appear in the New Testament. The absence of an anchor in the New Testament explains the selection of Luke 10 for the Gospel reading. These three Marian feasts rely on hymnography for their primary liturgical theology in a detour from the plan we are employing throughout this study.

The three Marian feasts relied upon the Church's memory in narrating their events. The Gospel of James (Protoevangelion), a second-century source on the life of Jesus possibly of Coptic provenance, provides the details on Mary's birth and entrance into the temple.[38] The Gospel of James depicts Mary's parents, Joachim and Anna, as pious Jews and faithful adherents of God's law. Mary's entrance into the temple not only fulfills the divine law but reveals her as one who desires to be in the Lord's presence by remaining in the temple. The Gospel of James does not mention the events surrounding Mary's death. The details on her death are found in diverse homilies dating from as early as the sixth century.

Many theologians of Christian late antiquity received these three stories as pillars of Christian tradition despite their absence from the New Testament. While the hymnography of the feasts provides summaries of the historical details, the hymns also explain the underpinning Christology and describe Mary's role as mediatrix of the church. In this sense, it is traditional Christology that shapes the meaning of these feasts. Mary's intercession functions as a salient secondary theme. The following examples of hymns taken from each of the three feasts illustrate both the foundational Christology and Mary's ministry. The claims made by the hymns are bold.

---

38. de Strycker, "Le Protévangile."

Theological Themes in Mary's Birth

The hymns of the feast of Mary's birth establish the pattern for the meaning of this feast. The liturgy makes bold claims about Mary's role in God's plan for the salvation of humankind. Mary's birth is not limited to the beginning of salvation, but she has a hand in releasing Adam and Eve from corruption and delivering humanity from death. The doxastikon at Vespers makes these claims, adding that Mary has also "made us godlike."[39] The troparion for the feast folds Christ's work into the commemoration of Mary's birth. The hymn claims that Mary's birth brings joy to the universe because she will give birth to Christ. It is Christ who has "loosed us from the curse" and granted us eternal life.[40]

The hymns illuminate Mary as someone extraordinary. She is preordained and chosen by God, and the hymns draw again from the Gospel of James by announcing that Joachim and Anna had been childless, Anna barren. The hymns imply an oft-repeated refrain threaded through much of the hymnographical corpus: "the barren woman bears the Theotokos who sustains our life."[41] The hymns frequently reflect on Mary as the antithesis of Eve, a convenient theme since the classical soteriological scheme attributes death to the disobedience of Adam and Eve. Mary's birth is included among the events that annulled the curse brought on by the human ancestors. The festal exaposteilarion exemplifies the claim that Mary's birth annuls Eve's curse. It is a universal feast, one celebrated by Christians "from the ends of the earth," and its cure is manifold. Mary's birth not only heals Anna's barrenness, but it also undoes the curse on childbirth that Eve brought upon herself.[42]

The feast of Mary's birth is the first major event at the beginning of the liturgical year, and it precedes a more elaborate celebration of the Exaltation of the Cross just six days later, on September 14.[43] The corpus of texts for Mary's birth occasionally refers to the upcoming feast. This has two purposes: practical, to preview the next major commemoration, and theological, to fold Mary's birth as an essential event into the larger scheme of salvation. Mary's birth is an instance of the expansion of the

39. *Festal Menaion*, 105.

40. *Festal Menaion*, 107.

41. See the kontakion and ikos, *Festal Menaion*, 119.

42. *Festal Menaion*, 125.

43. See, for example, the two katavasias on the second canon of Mary's birth in *Festal Menaion*, 125.

sequence of soteriological events in the church's memory through its appointment to the liturgical year.

Mary as Temple, Ark, and Fulfillment of the Law
in the Entrance Feast

The first sticheron at Vespers on "Lord, I have cried" defines Mary as both the ark and temple. The church venerates not the ark and tabernacle of the old covenant but Mary, who is now ark and tabernacle, since she is the one who "contained the word who cannot be contained."[44] This sticheron demonstrates the tendency of the Church to include the entirety of the mystery of the incarnation into a feast commemorating a sacred event. This is not merely a matter of Mary's piety—the Church venerates her for an event outside of the scope of the details of the entrance, as she is the God-bearer. Sound theology is the occasion for the feast—Mary is praised for her assent to God's plan, for the uncontainable one to make his dwelling among humankind.

The fourth sticheron at Vespers draws upon the piety the Gospel of James attributes to Mary and her family, Joachim and Anna. Mary loves the divine law so much that she lives in the temple. The Holy Spirit is the one who led her there, and an angel sustains her.[45] The hymn is catechetical; it reminds the liturgical participant of the details of Mary, her ever-virginity, and status as the true temple because she carried God in her womb.

The troparion defines the Entrance as the "herald of the salvation of men," similar to the message proclaimed by the troparion of Mary's Birth.[46] The hymns emphasize the need to praise and confess Mary as the Theotokos. The exaposteilarion of the feast exemplifies the need for a proper Mariology when it calls upon the assembly to praise "in faith, Mary the Child of God."[47] The hymn expresses Marian typology explicitly, claiming that the prophets spoke of her as a jar of manna, Aaron's rod, a tablet of the law, and an uncut mountain.[48] These liturgical exhortations to praise and confess Mary

44. *Festal Menaion*, 164.

45. "Led by the Holy Spirit, the holy Maid without spot is taken to dwell in the holy of holies. By an angel she is fed, who is in truth the most holy temple of our holy God," (*Festal Menaion*, 164).

46. *Festal Menaion*, 172.

47. *Festal Menaion*, 193.

48. *Festal Menaion*, 193.

are implicitly christological. The method is similar to the evangelical use of genealogies that place Christ as the heir and fulfillment of Adam, Abraham, and David. God was present in the divine law written by his hand in the old covenant. Mary is the vessel for making the new covenant in the flesh and is therefore an essential character in the soteriological narrative.

Confessing Mary as the legitimate tabernacle and ark is neither an end to itself, nor exclusively Mariological. When liturgical participants confess Mary as the true vessel of God in the flesh, they are also confessing their faith in Christ who is God. The hymns epitomize this unique feature of Marian feasts. They commemorate an event in history, but the entire feast itself refers to the mystery of Christ, so each Marian feast is actually christological. For our purposes, it is noteworthy that feasts become the primary markers for correct Orthodox theology.

Theological Themes from the Dormition Feast

The Dormition has been a topic of study in the theological academy because of the development of Mariology in the Roman Catholic Church. Catholic theologians studied the Eastern Christian tradition of the Dormition in the process leading up to Pope Pius XII's apostolic constitution *Munificentissimus Deus*. For Roman Catholics, this teaching is infallible, belonging to the extraordinary magisterium seldom employed by popes. The Catholic teaching on the Assumption of Mary is similar to the Dormition with one significant difference. The Assumption doctrine does not explicitly state that Mary died, whereas Mary clearly died in Orthodoxy's Dormition narrative.

The Dormition itself is significant in its own rite. This is the sole Marian feast to have a fast, which occurs two weeks prior to it.[49] The fast is the last of the four to appear on the Orthodox liturgical calendar. The cycle of Dormition services is more extensive than those of the other Marian feasts. The order consists of the usual cycle of the Hours, but the Vigil deviates from the customary pattern and includes lamentations sung before a tomb of Mary and an epitaphios bearing her icon. The Dormition

---

49. See Tkachenko, "Год Церковный." The Christmas fast is forty days and was established in the ninth and tenth centuries; the Apostles' fast begins on the Monday after the first Sunday after Pentecost and lasts until June 28 and was also established in the ninth and tenth centuries; the Dormition fast is fourteen days and was established in the twelfth and thirteenth centuries.

follows the blueprint of the Matins and Lamentations of Holy Saturday. The liturgy completes the cycle.

The hymns appointed to the Dormition provide the primary sources of its theology. They recall the gathering of the apostles at Mary's death and the glorious character of her translation from earth to heaven. She commends her soul to Christ himself, and her journey to heaven inaugurates her eternal ministry of intercession for the church. The doxastikon on the lity at the Vigil expresses all of these themes, threaded throughout the entire service.[50] The hymn claims that heaven is "opened wide" to receive Mary, who is "translated from life to life."[51] It concludes with a petition to Mary to not forget her "ties of kinship" to the church as she goes to heaven.[52]

Mary's role in heaven is that of mediator. The first apostichon of the feast explicates this ministry, asking her to entreat Christ for the salvation of souls.[53] The hypakoe on the canon blesses Mary for her intercessions and supplications that strengthen the "scepters of kings."[54] The hymns assert that Christ himself comes to escort Mary to eternal life.[55] Apostles, angels, and Christ escort Mary to heaven for her ministry of intercession. A troparion on "Ode 7" of the second canon states that "the queen goes to dwell with her son and to rule with him forever."[56]

The implications of these theological themes are multilayered. Mary's death was a marvelous event, a mystery, because of the extraordinary events leading up to her translation to heaven. The apostles and the angels are gathered to witness the event by the power of God. Christ escorts Mary to heaven and receives her there. Mary continues her ministry of intercession and supplication for the church, but she is also glorified, dwells with God, and rules with her son.

The Dormition expresses some of the themes characteristic of sanctoral feasts. Mediating for one's native community is an early and staple

50. Tkachenko, "Год Церковный."

51. Tkachenko, "Год Церковный."

52. Tkachenko, "Год Церковный."

53. Tkachenko, "Год Церковный."

54. Tkachenko, "Год Церковный."

55. See, for example, the first troparion on the ninth ode of the first canon of the feast. The hymn states that the angelic powers marveled at the sight of Christ (their "Master") "bearing in his hands the soul of a woman" and inviting her to "be glorified together" with the Father and the Son (Tkachenko, "Год Церковный").

56. Tkachenko, "Год Церковный."

feature of the lives of saints.[57] God grants forgiveness to the community gathered in memory of a saint through the holy one's intercessions, as Peter Brown has argued.[58] Mary's Dormition is not limited to a ministry of intercession, however. The hymns accurately portray it as a mystery. It is a paschal event; she departs the earthly life to begin the heavenly, and she receives the gift of glorification and the dignity of regency. This is a bold claim; Mary experiences Christ's Pascha, passing through death to life, with her translation to heaven resembling his ascension.

The framework of the story of Mary's Dormition is fairly clear. The feast follows the pattern of Holy Week, with the obvious but important distinction in the manner of Mary's death. The theological claim is significant. Christ's ascension into heaven meant that a human being lived in eternal communion with God. Mary's Dormition follows this blueprint; she, too, lives together with God. Mary's passage from death to glorified life is a seal of God's promise of resurrection to humankind. The Dormition is the solemnity of Mary's Pascha, a Pascha belonging to a secondary rhythm of the liturgical year's fixed cycle.

---

57. Brown, *Cult of the Saints*, 41.

58. Brown, *Cult of the Saints*, 92–96.

The Annunciation: A Major Feast in Lent

While the Annunciation is one of the four core Marian commemorations, we treat it independently because of its connections to the incarnation cycle. It was celebrated in Constantinople possibly as early as the fifth century, the date of March 25 was codified during the reign of Justinian in the sixth century, along with Christmas and the Hypapante.[59] The significance of the dates revives the crucial function of the solar rhythms governing the year. The

59. Taft and Carr, "Annunciation."

Lukan account states that the Annunciation occurred six months after the conception of John the Baptist (Luke 1:26). This coincided with the autumn equinox, so Jesus' conception takes place at the spring equinox.[60]

The Orthodox observance of the Annunciation occasionally entails complex variations on liturgical celebrations, especially since Pascha is still observed on the Julian (old) calendar. It always takes place after Lent has started and can occur during Holy Week or even on Pascha (known then as Kyriopascha). When the Annunciation falls during Lent, a Divine Liturgy is celebrated with Vespers, the lone exception to the rule of having a liturgy on a weekday of Lent. As the book illustrating how the church governs the convergence of commemorations, the typikon lists no less than ten scenarios for the coincidence of the Annunciation with the weeks of Lent, the days of Holy Week, and Pascha.[61]

Technically, the Annunciation is a Marian feast. Many of the Marian themes explored in the three other core feasts appear here as well. For example, the second sticheron of the lity at Vigil folds Mary into the soteriological scheme by identifying her as the restoration of Adam and the deliverance of Eve.[62] The hymns employ paradox to play on Mary as the antithesis of Eve, with Gabriel the opposite of the serpent.[63] In fact, many of the hymns recreate a complete dialogue between Gabriel and Mary, especially the canons assigned to the feast.

The outstanding theme of the feast is joy in the incarnation. The hymns express this joy repeatedly. The doxastikon of the stichera on the praises is among the most poignant expressions of incarnational joy in the language of Orthodox christological doctrine. The hymn calls upon creation and nature to rejoice because the "Son of God becomes the son of man" and, in so doing, makes it possible for humanity to partake of the life of God.[64]

---

60. Talley, *Origins of the Liturgical Year*, 8–13, 91–103.

61. See the list in *Festal Menaion*, 435–37.

62. *Festal Menaion*, 442.

63. "Once the serpent beguiled Eve, but now I announce to thee the good tidings of joy!" (*Festal Menaion*, 444). Quote is from the doxastikon of the lity when the feast falls upon a Saturday or Sunday.

64. *Festal Menaion*, 460. The third sticheron on the praises is even more theologically profound, announcing that the "coeternal Word of the Father without beginning" has come down to become human (*Festal Menaion*, 459).

Summary Observations on the Marian Cycle of Feasts

The four core feasts of the Marian cycle are multifunctional. The feasts represent the expansion of the liturgical year and Christian flexibility to designate events that are not recorded by the New Testament as major solemnities, as long as they are part of the church's memory. The Marian feasts are expansive in another way, by extending the soteriological scheme to underscore the importance of Mary's assent to give birth to Christ. Mary contributes to the salvation of humankind because of her agreement to participate in God's plan. It is for this reason that the feasts praise Mary and call upon the church to honor her while also celebrating the mystery of Christ as the heart of each. Essentially, the church shows how secondary characters in God's grand narrative illuminate the gift of salvation to humankind. At their core, the Marian feasts point to Christ and ultimately reveal his mystery and that of his incarnation and Pascha.

It is essential to acknowledge that the Marian feasts are products of the rapid and substantial *déroulement* of Marian piety from the fifth century onwards. The feasts call upon the faithful to honor Mary above all others, even the angels. She exercises a ministry exclusive to her, becoming an intercessor for Christians by pleading for them at God's throne. A number of factors contributed to Mary's exaltation in Christianity, and her titles and ministry—including ruling with Christ as queen—represent the influence of Christian piety. The festal exhortation to honor her often takes on a life of its own and detaches from the narrative that presents Mary as referring all to Christ. In other words, the feasts become about Mary only, even if this is not the pastoral intention.

This examination of the Marian feasts demonstrates that the incarnational and paschal undercurrents remain in place. A simple pastoral correction is both possible and desirable. The solution is to embrace Mary as an essential but secondary character in the story. The narratives are not about Mary but ultimately remind the faithful that Mary, along with her parents Joachim and Anna, are also faithful disciples. As a secondary character, Mary provides a model for Christians to adopt and follow. She does not replace Christ as the mediator before God's throne but adds her petitions. Mary also functions as a female model of Christian discipleship to be adopted by all Christians, regardless of gender identity.

John the Baptist: Another Secondary Character

The Orthodox calendar has several feasts of John the Baptist. These are connected to the incarnation and Marian cycle because of the Lukan account. John's birth is appointed to June 24, the summer equinox, and just over six months prior to the birth of Christ. This places the feast of his conception on September 23. The Church commemorates John's death (beheading) on August 29 with a strict fast day. John's birth and beheading are designated as great feasts in the typikon.[65] There are also liturgical commemorations of the finding of John's head, and the synaxis devoted to his memory on January 7, the day after Theophany.

The hymnography of the feasts employs some of the same literary flourishes discussed in the Marian feasts earlier. The commemoration of the synaxis of John the Baptist on January 7 is a good example. The hymns fold John into the soteriological scheme as demonstrated by the troparion, which claims that John "preached also to those in hell the good tidings of God made manifest in the flesh."[66] The feasts of John depend upon the biblical patterns of divine intervention through conception that appear in the birth of Christ and Mary. The troparion for the feast of John's birth (June 24) expresses joy at John's birth for ending his father's silence and his

65. Typikon, 704, 813.
66. *Festal Menaion*, 392.

mother's barrenness.[67] Jesus, Mary, and John have similar cycles of feasts inscribed on the liturgical calendar and presented in Table 3.6.

Table 3.6: Cycles of Jesus, Mary, John

	Jesus	Mary	John
Conception	March 25	December 9	September 23
Birth	December 25	September 8	June 24
Death (resurrection, translation)	Movable Cycle	August 15	August 29

The entire Marian cycle is not recorded in the New Testament but is observed on the liturgical calendar. The inclusion of this cycle of feasts for Christ and the two most prominent secondary characters of the New Testament (Mary and John) represents the liturgical tendencies identified earlier: the expansion of the liturgical calendar to include significant markers in the life cycle of important figures, such as the conception of Mary by Anna and John by Elizabeth, and the coincidence of these feasts with the solar equinoxes. This coincidence forms one of the pillars of the liturgical year and its sense of seasonality. The specific dates warrant one final observation: only Jesus' conception and birth amount to a perfect nine months. The conceptions of Mary and John are slightly imperfect, differentiating them from Jesus. This discrepancy functions as an important difference between the Orthodox and Roman Catholic Church for Marian observances.

Fitting in: Transfiguration and the Exaltation of the Cross

Two holidays remain from the cycle of great feasts observed in Orthodoxy: the Transfiguration on August 6 and the Exaltation of the Cross on September 14. The historical origins of the Transfiguration feast are somewhat uncertain. One hypothesis is that the dedication of three churches on Mount Tabor inspired the annual commemoration of the Transfiguration.[68] The Georgian Lectionary (fifth to eighth centuries) includes an entry for it with

67. See the festal Troparion at https://www.oca.org/saints/troparia/2017/06/24/101800-nativity-of-the-holy-glorious-prophet-forerunner-and-baptist-joh (accessed February 15, 2022).

68. Podskalsky, Taft, and Carr, "Transfiguration."

readings from the prophecies of Amos and Zechariah, 1 Peter, Hebrews, and Matthew.[69] The likelihood of its hagiopolitan provenance suggests that Constantinople adopted it from Jerusalem. The feast is established on the Constantinopolitan calendar by the ninth or tenth century, evidenced by the Typikon of the Great Church.[70]

The Exaltation of the Cross originated as the feast of dedication of the Anastasis Church in Jerusalem in the fourth century, accompanied by St. Helena's finding of the cross.[71] In Jerusalem, the dedication feast took place on September 13 and the veneration of the cross in the Martyrium Church occurred the following day (September 14). Daniel Galadza shows that the commemoration of the cross superseded the dedication commemoration by the eleventh century.[72]

While these two feasts were inspired historically by a sense of sacred topography, they became connected fixtures on the liturgical calendar. The Gospels for the Transfiguration are taken from Luke (9:28–36) and Matthew (17:1–9), and the epistle is 2 Peter 1:10–19. The hymns appointed to it have two primary themes: the appearance of the divine light in Christ and the anticipation of the forthcoming feast of the cross on September 14. The third aposticho at vigil mentions the "overwhelming flood" of Christ's divine light that the three disciples beheld.[73] A troparion on the first canon of the feast expresses Orthodox Christology, stating that the "nature that knows no change" was revealed to the disciples in some "small measure."[74] The ikos exhorts the faithful to approach Christ in the form of a "divine ascent."[75]

The connections to the Exaltation of the Cross are threaded throughout the order of services. The first two stichera of vespers have the same beginning, "before Thy crucifixion, o Lord."[76] The hermoi for the canon for the Exaltation of the Cross are sung as the katavasia for the festal

---

69. *Le Grand Lectionnaire,* nos. 1126–33, 25.

70. Mateos, *Typicon,* vol. 1, 360–63.

71. See Galadza, *Liturgy and Byzantinization,* 244–46.

72. Galadza, *Liturgy and Byzantinization,* 245.

73. *Festal Menaion,* 477. A second sessional hymn at Matins is more explicit, referring to Christ's revelation of his hidden and blinding light to the disciples (*Festal Menaion,* 479–80).

74. *Festal Menaion,* 487.

75. *Festal Menaion,* 488.

76. *Festal Menaion,* 470.

canon at vigil, a clear marker of connecting the two feasts. These liturgical cues are not manufactured, since the Gospel accounts have Jesus foretelling the crucifixion at the end of the episode on Tabor (e.g., Matt 17:9, the last verse of the liturgy gospel). Forty days separate the Transfiguration from the Exaltation, a traditional period of preparation. The forty-day period is not, however, one of strict fasting. The day of the Exaltation itself requires a strict fast, but in the current scheme, the Transfiguration occurs during the two-week period of the Dormition fast. The Gospel account itself functions as the source of the connection between the Transfiguration and the Exaltation.

The Exaltation of the Cross has essentially become one of the three primary commemorations of the cross and Christ's death in the liturgical year. It accompanies the movable solemnities of the Sunday of the Cross (third of Lent) and Good Friday. The preparation for the feast reveals its degree of its solemnity, as special psalmody and readings are appointed to the Saturdays and Sundays before and after it. The readings are compatible with the general theme of the cross. The first Old Testament reading from Exodus (15:2–16:1) recounts Moses throwing a tree into the bitter waters of Marah to quench the people's thirst. The second reading from Proverbs (3:1–11) pairs with the epistle (1 Cor 1:18–24) to reveal the cross as the fulfillment of the manifestation of God's wisdom. The Gospel from John consists of select passages from Jesus' crucifixion and death.

The hymns appointed to the feast reveal the occasion as centered on the relic of the cross. Many of the hymns address the cross—"Hail! Lifegiving cross," "O precious cross"—and then define it as an instrument of victory over adversaries.[77] The hymnographers incorporated bellicose vocabulary in their praise of the cross, referring to it as a trophy, a weapon, and an instrument of victory over enemies visible and invisible, past and present.[78] The collection of hymns reveals the cross as the instrument of reconciliation with God, a shield of protection from enemies, and a weapon to defeat the empire's enemies. George Demacopoulos asserts that some of the hymns evince a sacralization of violence and a fusion of Roman political ideology with Orthodox ecclesiology.[79] The feast, therefore,

77. These exhortations are threaded throughout the hymns appointed to the day.

78. These themes permeate many of the hymns. See, for example, the hymns attributed to emperor Leo that exhort the people to come forward and venerate the cross in *Festal Menaion*, 156.

79. Demacopoulos, "Feast of the Exaltation," unpublished essay. I am grateful to Dr. Demacopoulos for sharing his essay with me.

has multiple purposes. The primary theme of triumph is in homage to Constantine and the Roman emperors defending the Christian Empire.[80] The hymns refer to multiple instances of Old Testament figures making the gesture of the sign of the cross as antecedents. The most repeated Old Testament scene is taken from Exodus 17, when Moses holds his arms outstretched so the Hebrews can defeat the Amalekites.[81] The repetitive references of the hymns to victory, Christian triumphalism, and regency—to the point of referring to Christ as king—disclose the original inspiration for this feast. It is a celebration of the finding and elevation of the relic of the cross first and foremost, and this theme supersedes the secondary and tertiary ones of Christ's victory over death.

The Exaltation feast includes an elaborate and dramatic rite of the elevation of the cross with the singing of "Lord, Have Mercy" five hundred times, one hundred for each time the presider elevates the cross and faces each of the four directions. Some parishes do not include this rite in the festal observances, as it is most frequently celebrated under episcopal presidency. The rite expresses cosmic Christian triumphalism, facing four directions to indicate the cross's victory over the world, and the relic and act of veneration of the cross as the primary purpose of the feast.

The Transfiguration and Exaltation feasts round out the most solemn feasts of the Orthodox liturgical year. Both are inspired by the dedication of churches, sacred topography, and relics. Sacred topography was an important element of the development of the liturgical year in Jerusalem. The veneration of relics becomes the primary ingredient in the continued population of feasts on the annual calendar. The Exaltation is one of the earliest and most solemn examples of this phenomenon, and we will treat the continuation of this pattern in the next chapter.

This review of the Transfiguration and Exaltation feasts raises a question on the synergy of these feasts with the rest of the liturgical year. If they originated as themes associated with sacred topography and the anniversary of the finding of a relic, what is their significance in the liturgical year? The Synoptic Gospels place Jesus' Transfiguration on Mount Tabor before his crucifixion, a significant event foreshadowing Pascha. The additional commemoration of the Transfiguration as the second Sunday of Lent in the

80. See, for example, the third sticheron on the praises, containing a passage that says, "by the cross barbarian nations are conquered, by the cross the sceptres of kings are confirmed," (Demacopoulos, "Feast of the Exaltation," 153).

81. See, for example, hymns on the lity on 128, 129, and of the aposticha on 140. Note that Exodus 17 is not included in the cursus of readings appointed to the feast.

Roman Church is sensible in terms of its organic connection with Pascha.[82] The Orthodox Church has not implemented this reform.

For Orthodoxy, then, the Transfiguration feast has two purposes. First, it is a feast of revelation, an occasion to proclaim the church's Christology. Second, there is the matter of the evangelical synergy of the Transfiguration with Pascha. This synergy makes it convenient to begin singing the hymns of the Exaltation on the Transfiguration despite the fact that the historical and thematic origins of the respective feasts are mutually exclusive. Lev Gillet's remarks on the blessings received by the people on the Transfiguration illuminate its second purpose. Gillet observes that the conversation of Moses and Elijah with Jesus about the passion deserves more attention.[83] He states that the faithful's Transfiguration is inexorably caught up with the carrying of the cross.[84] In other words, we can be truly transformed only when we accept the crosses God brings to us. Gillet's explanation of the Transfiguration provides a new perspective on the synergy between the Transfiguration and the Exaltation.

The themes of Christian universalism and venerating the relic of the cross supersede the core message of the Exaltation. These messages are simply not transferable to the post-imperial cultural and pastoral environments no matter how creatively one manipulates the hymnographical material. The presence of paschal and incarnational themes in Theophany and the Marian feasts suggest a pastoral solution for presiders and parishes. It is appropriate to honor the cross and commemorate Jesus' Pascha during any time of the liturgical year. The readings assigned to the Exaltation facilitate the possibility of celebrating the Exaltation on September 14, a late summer feast of the cross.

Conclusion

The overview of the fixed cycle of the Orthodox liturgical year yields a number of observations and issues. Several factors contribute to the growth of the calendar. These include solar events, historical mimesis, theological development, sacred topography, and the dedication of

---

82. See *Roman Missal*, 226–29. Protestants using the Revised Common Lectionary celebrate Transfiguration Sunday as the last Sunday after the Epiphany. See, for example, *Evangelical Lutheran Worship*, 25–26.

83. A Monk of the Eastern Church, *Year of Grace*, 240.

84. A Monk of the Eastern Church, *Year of Grace*, 241.

churches. A significant outcome of the pattern of liturgical development is liturgical expansion, the gradual appearance of several mini-cycles expressing numerous themes.

The incarnation feasts constitute the first smaller cycle, especially when Christmas was affixed to the existing pattern of Theophany and the Meeting forty days later. Theology was a primary inspiration for these feasts, and Theophany also had salient paschal features, especially because of its close association with baptism. The emergence of synaxes of prominent secondary characters in the stories—Mary (December 26), John the Baptist (January 7), and Simeon and Anna (February 3)—epitomize the impact of veneration for secondary characters on the liturgical expansion of mini-cycles.

Theology and the cult of saints along with some sacred topography inspired the development of the Marian cycle. This cycle of feasts is also important because of its dependence on and reference to the blueprint of feasts of Christ. The Dormition occupies a venerable position with its promise of resurrection from the dead for all of humankind expressed by the rites and hymnography. The Marian feasts also demonstrate how trends in popular piety become affixed to the liturgical year, with Mary's mediation for the church a clear demonstration of this phenomenon.

The equinoxes of the solar cycle and the powerful memories of local events were significant factors in the determination of the liturgical year. The equinoxes functioned as magnets for feasts and facilitated pastoral explanations of Christ as the light of the world or spring as a time of rebirth that are compatible with the themes of light, darkness, death, and resurrection. When the anniversaries of the dedication of churches become permanent fixtures in the annual cycle, they evince the power of community memory. The only reason for communities to gather on the anniversary of a specific event is on account of its deep penetration into the people's identity. The intensity of festal solemnity increases over time as the memory of the figure becomes more precious for the native community. Community memory is perhaps the most formidable aspect of the liturgical year—even more so than the concept of time itself.

The outcome of these factors, many of which occurred repeatedly, was a fixed cycle consisting of mini-cycles of feasts that often overlapped with one another. It can be difficult for pastors to make sense of these amalgamations, and the truth is that there is no single principle providing the rhythm or reason for the structure of the annual fixed cycle. The church used innovative methods to try to govern overlapping themes, especially through the creation of a typikon. The many variants of the Annunciation demonstrate this governance clearly.

Two issues confront pastors as they formulate plans for navigating this fixed cycle of the liturgical year. The first is practical and concerns the kind of ordo the pastor should observe. The second is more complex. How does the pastor make sense of the multiple convergences and themes presented by the historical development of the liturgical year?

Orthodoxy has handled the first issue through multiple methods. Many pastors observe the principle of converting the people to the established liturgical order. This method entails serving most or all of the liturgical offices appointed to each festal cycle, regardless of attendance. Others revise the liturgy to conform to the people's lives. The appointment of vesperal festal liturgies offered on the eve of a feast is the most innovative attempt to address this issue. The faithful are able to both hear the story of the feast and partake in its fullness through Holy Communion. Some church officials have resisted this approach and have attempted to stifle it. The issue will continue to be divisive until pastors agree on the rigidity of the ordo. Some view the prescribed liturgical ordos of the typikon as akin to liturgical law. Others view the typikon as providing a blueprint that should be adapted by the pastor to conform to the realities of his parish.

The second issue is initiating the people into the rhythm and flow of the liturgical year. While much of the liturgical year is self-explanatory, it can be difficult to explain the numerous convergences and occasionally opaque liturgical material. The Exaltation is a good example. This feast echoes the era of messianic imperialism, the utopia of a Christian empire that defeats adversarial neighbors under the banner of the cross. In this particular example, the hymnography deviates from the primary liturgical theology of the appointed lessons. The Exaltation occasions the principle for preaching and teaching the liturgical year to be adopted by pastors, who draw exclusively from the appointed lessons to explain what the assembly is celebrating on that day. No secondary level of explanation should be necessary. In this instance, one possible theme is to explain that the cross, as the center of Christian faith, is celebrated in word and rite at all levels of the liturgical year: Sunday, and the movable and fixed cycles.

Marian feasts present a more formidable challenge for the simple reason that Mary's birth, entrance into the temple, and death are not recorded in the New Testament. These feasts in particular provide a good opportunity to connect the appointed scriptural lessons with the community traditions that commemorated them. The church embraced a selection of narratives on Mary's life that were never added to the canonical New Testament. Pastors have an opportunity to remind the people that God is continually acting and that Scripture is the most important component of tradition but not the only one.

The inner synergy of the liturgical year presents a substantial opportunity for pastoral liturgy. Marian feasts are not reducible to Mary but invite the people to join her in worshipping Christ. It is also possible to celebrate the paschal mystery through and with other secondary characters of the New Testament like Mary and John. The fluidity of the liturgical year honors the wholeness of the mystery of Christ himself. It is right to celebrate his Pascha on any day even if that occasion honors one of his disciples.

4

Everything Else

THE ORTHODOX LITURGICAL YEAR includes several feasts and commemorations of varying ranks that are important in parish life. Saints' days are significant, and a number of feasts have developed around the lives of the saints. These include occasions of miracles worked by saints through relics, such as Mary's belt, or a number of wonder-working icons. The calendar also features commemorations of the holy angels (especially Michael and Gabriel), and epic events in church history.

The liturgical celebration of saints and events illuminates the synergy between the local and the universal. Commemorations of the ecumenical councils and saints like the apostles Peter and Paul, Ignatius of Antioch, and Nicholas of Myra have reasonably intense observances at the universal level. Commemorations of specific events and saints are often local phenomena. Figures such as Nino of Georgia, Sava of Serbia, and Sergius of Radonezh, and events like the Baptism of Rus' hold special significance in local places, while they are known universally.

A number of secondary liturgical rites have developed around the commemorations of saints and relics. Those who are named after saints are honored on the day of the saint's feast in significant domestic commemorations of name's days. In the Serbian tradition, the name's day becomes a rather elaborate domestic rite called a *slava*.

A number of other extraliturgical and domestic rites are also deeply meaningful for the people. Extraliturgical rites include the blessing of paschal baskets, fruit on the Transfiguration, and flowers on the Dormition. House blessings (associated with the Theophany on January 6) and the *Sviata Vechera* (Holy Supper) of Christmas are examples of domestic rites. Some of these rites are folded into the liturgy and have prayers appointed by the church, whereas others do not belong to the official liturgical tradition yet are central to the meaning of the feast.

This chapter's presentation on "everything else" presents two primary issues. First is the tendency for solemn feasts to produce secondary and tertiary liturgical offices. We have already seen examples of the expansion of a major feast with the synaxes following the incarnational feasts. In the sanctoral cycle, commemorations of miracles performed through relics and icons are examples of secondary and tertiary expansion. Second is the parallel and related emergence of domestic celebrations around feasts appointed to the liturgical year. These rites evoke the long-standing question of the relationship between public liturgy and private devotion, but our concern is not to reassert the proper hierarchy of liturgy superseding devotions. Rather, we will examine domestic practices in an attempt to understand why they became so prominent and how they relate to the official, public liturgical rites.

Saints' Days: The Model for All Feasts

We have already referred to the influence of saints' days on the development of the Marian calendar. Paul Bradshaw and Maxwell Johnson assert that local churches began to maintain lists of martyrs and saints and celebrated the anniversary of their deaths with a Eucharist on their tombs in the third century, on the basis of epistolary evidence from Cyprian of Carthage.[1] The martyr's anniversary of their death was their *dies natalis* or birthday into the kingdom of God. The Roman *depositio martyrium* presents an early witness to the listing of saints' feast days, part of the Chronograph of 354.[2] Bradshaw and Johnson emphasize the significance of the hagiographical narrative of Polycarp with its obvious connection to the Eucharist.[3] Polycarp exemplifies the early Christian pattern of veneration of a local saint by gathering at the tomb for the celebration of the Eucharist. This pattern, originally coalescing around the intimate memory of a beloved martyr, became a blueprint for the lives of saints in general, one that came to influence the trajectory of the lives of saints and the liturgical year in the churches of both the West and East. In addition to the literary significance of the saint's vita, the liturgy had ritual and spatial implications.

1. Bradshaw and Johnson, *Origins of Feasts*, 174.
2. Bradshaw and Johnson, *Origins of Feasts*, 175.
3. Bradshaw and Johnson, *Origins of Feasts*, 177–79.

Eucharistic liturgies celebrated on the graves of the saints transformed the grave into an altar. Polycarp's vita has eucharistic overtones, and a saint's grave is similar to Christ's, a sacred place where death is translated to life. Local communities continued to gather at the location of their saint's burial site, and Eucharists celebrated at the grave eventually provided the inspiration for erecting buildings on the burial site.

Early church architecture captured the spirit of celebrating the Eucharist at the grave site through the *martyrium*, a small cemetery chapel housing the body of the saint.[4] In his classic study on the topic, Peter Brown states that the celebration of a saint was a communal event involving the people of the city or town.[5] The saint's burial site provided a gathering place for the people's assembly, and ancillary events developed around the official rituals associated with the saint.

The phenomenon of the veneration of saints and their annual commemoration often transcended the boundaries of the local community. A powerful sense of sacred topography emerged in the milieu of the saint's burial site, and the saint's body and possessions. The saint had been welcomed into God's kingdom, so the remnants of the saint on earth—their body and possessions—were consecrated and regarded with an esteem similar to the Eucharist itself.[6]

The presence of the holy in tangible, touchable things, such as the body, clothing, possessions, and texts, attracted not only natives intimately familiar with the life of the saint, but also pilgrims. Christians regarded saints as trustworthy intercessors before God's throne and prayed to them for intercession. Praying for saints as part of the communion sanctorum was—and remains—part of the Christian tradition, as argued by Bradshaw and Johnson.[7] They refer to the prayers for the saints and the Theotokos during the anaphora of the Divine Liturgy as evidence, rooted in a tradition traceable to the fourth century. Praying to the saints for their intercession was also a part of the Christian tradition, evidenced as early as the second century.[8]

It is not difficult to see how the intimate gathering of a local community at a saint's grave on the anniversary of their death led to the gradual

4. See Devonshire Jones et al., "Martyrium."

5. Adam, *Liturgical Year*, 207.

6. Bradshaw and Johnson, *Origins of Feasts*, 179.

7. Bradshaw and Johnson, *Origins of Feasts*, 180.

8. Bradshaw and Johnson, *Origins of Feasts*, 180–82.

adoption of the local saint in other places. Pilgrims visiting the grave of the saint and participating in the local liturgy shared news of the power of the event. The local bishops would give away a relic of the saint to a fellow bishop in a gesture of Christian hospitality, a practice that became known as the transfer of relics. Christian churches of other locations came to adopt a saint and would commemorate them on their appointed anniversary on the liturgical calendar. The transfer of relics became one of the vehicles through which local saints came to be universally commemorated. The practice was and remains prevalent in the East. Receiving and installing relics of a saint from another place enabled the migration of the saint's presence into the new place. The process of venerating saints in designated places experienced a gradual transformation. The first stage surrounded the saint's grave, which functioned simultaneously as an altar for the Eucharist. In the second stage, church structures were built upon the burial site, with the altar above the crypt.

In early Roman churches, clergy could gain access to the relics of the saint resting in the *confessio,* a shrine that was accessible via a passage connecting the sanctuary to the shrine.[9] In the next stage, and also in current practice, saintly relics were installed within the altar table during the dedication of churches.[10] It is also customary to sew holy relics into the antimension, a cloth that functions like a portable altar. The antimension bears the bishop's signature and is essentially a certificate that permits and legitimizes community life, organization, and the blessing for the priest to preside at the Divine Liturgy and other divine services. Some parishes also have relics encased on their own and in small compartments that also hold the icon of saint(s). Some cathedrals and monasteries have elaborate shrines displaying saintly relics and icons that are large enough to venerate during public liturgies and private devotions.

The preceding paragraph is an apt illustration of liturgical overgrowth. Saintly veneration began with communal Eucharists at the burial site and evolved into a standard system of transferring and installing relics. The process became so elaborate and solemn that installing relics in the altar or antimension became part of the requirement for a community's Divine Liturgy. This intricate instance of liturgical development

9. Allen Doig describes some examples of the *confessio.* See Doig, *Liturgy and Architecture,* 7, 26.

10. The seventh ecumenical council in Nicaea stipulated this practice in canon 7. See Tanner, *Decrees of the Ecumenical Councils,* vol. 1, 144–45.

has informative consequences for our interpretation of the liturgical year that warrant theological analysis.

First, the liturgical veneration of saints is both parallel to and dependent upon the ritual dynamics of the evolution of the feasts of Christ. The original feasts of Christ follow the patterns established by sacred topography and narrative. Palm Sunday, Holy Week, and Pascha are centered upon the events that occurred in Jerusalem and the narratives describing them. The Jordan River is the locus of the Theophany, and the accompanying narrative provides the basis for an annual commemoration. For saints' feasts, sacred topography and the hagiographical narrative follow the same pattern. The church originally assembled at the saint's burial site and celebrated their life through a narrative passed on via oral tradition. The similarity of Polycarp's vita with early eucharistic prayers shows that the liturgical forms of Christ's feast provided a blueprint for sanctoral celebrations.

The second point is significant for the received tradition of the liturgical year in Orthodoxy. Sanctoral celebrations were originally local phenomena, a gathering of the community in thankful memory of their beloved saint. The local became universal through pilgrimage, and the transfer of relics enabled the migration of sacred topography to other locations of the Christian world. One might describe this aspect of saintly commemoration as making saints tangible through their possessions. Bone fragments, clothing, and possessions made saints tangible, physically accessible to other Christian communities.

Iconography followed this pattern. Local icons established prototypes that could be copied. Essentially, the translation of relics and the ease of disseminating a viable hagiographical narrative made it possible for sacred topography to become mobile. The implications for heortology are significant. The universal liturgical commemoration of a saint limits the temporal dimension of the celebration. Each community's saintly feast recreates the community's space into the sacred topography of the saint. By commemorating the saint and reciting the appointed liturgical narratives celebrating their life, the Holy Spirit makes the saint present to the community, no matter who or where they are.

In other words, the feast itself is epicletic—the location of each celebrating community is now holy because of saintly presence and the grace of the divine act. This reality does not diminish the intensity of the celebration in the saint's native location—this remains an important factor in popular Orthodox piety. Nevertheless, it is certainly true that the writing and translation of hymns based on hagiographical narratives, the transfer of relics, and iconographic prototypes enhanced the migration of sacred topography and enlivened saints' days in Orthodoxy.

Categories of Saintly Commemoration

The Orthodox Church appoints saints into numerous categories. These include apostles, prophets, martyrs, confessors, healers, ascetics, monastics, and hierarchs.[11] A number of saintly categories reveal aspects of holiness that are similar to a primary category, including equal-to-the-apostles and passion-bearers. A few saints are identified as fools-for-Christ, people whose subversive acts expose the evils and vices of the world in comparison with the call to repentance and the coming of God's kingdom.

The ranking of saints is not always a significant factor in parish liturgical life. Only the Marian cycle and the saints commemorated on Sundays of Lent (Gregory Palamas, Mary of Egypt, and John Climacus) are observed universally among the Orthodox. A selection of saints' days are fixtures on the liturgical calendar. The feast of the apostles Peter and Paul (June 29), Nicholas (December 6), and the holy three hierarchs—Basil the Great, John Chrysostom, and Gregory the Theologian (January 30)—are observed in all Orthodox churches. So are the feasts of St. Michael and the Archangels (November 8), and St. George (April 23). A fast prepares the church for the feast of the apostles Peter and Paul. The fixed date is often close to Pentecost, so the fast-free octave of Pentecost often eliminates many days from the apostles' feast.

The Feast of All Saints

The dynamic of the universal and the local appears again in the commemoration of all saints. The Orthodox Church celebrates all saints on the first Sunday after Pentecost, unlike the churches of the West, which observe it on November 1.[12] The observance of all saints on the first Sunday of Pentecost makes the annual date movable, dependent on the calculation of Pascha.

11. Ware, *Orthodox Church*, 247–53; McGuckin, *Orthodox Church*, 222–34.

12. See Adam, *Liturgical Year*, 228–30 for an overview of the history of all saints in Rome. See Getcha, *Typikon Decoded,* 280–83 for a brief exposition of the Orthodox observation.

The title for this Sunday in the Typikon of the Great Church mentions all saints and the victorious martyrs.[13]

Like the first Sundays of Lent and Pascha, this Sunday is prestigious. Reserving the first Sunday after Pentecost for the victorious martyrs was compatible with the Byzantine preference for order (taxis).[14] The reference to the victorious martyrs reveals a potential theological reason for the appointment of this feast. New Christians receive the gift of the spirit at baptism and anointing. Martyrdom is the ultimate Christian act of witnessing, one that brings even an unbaptized person into covenantal communion with Christ.[15] In this sense, the commemoration of all saints has an organic connection to the feast of Pentecost.

Lev Gillet's reflection on the significance of the feast of All Saints for the life of the faithful is noteworthy. The Gospel appointed to the Sunday of All Saints is a composite from Matthew (10:32–33, 37–38; 19:27–30). The message is clear—Christians must renounce everything, including family connections, to be his disciples. The message introduces three realities. The first is obvious—God sends the Holy Spirit for Christians to be the body of Christ in everyday life, in service for the life of the world. The second is quite jarring following fifty days of rejoicing—the good news that he is risen brings the faithful back to their own crosses. Gillet explains that the disciples struggled mightily with Jesus' teachings until his ascent.[16] They did not truly embark on the difficult apostolic work of the cross until they had been filled with the fire of the Holy Spirit. In other words, it is that very fire that enables Christians to carry these crosses even when they require hard personal renunciations.

The Commemoration of All Saints of a Local Church

We move from the universal to the local with the commemoration of all saints at a local church. The annual commemoration of all saints in Russia is an illustrative example. The idea for the commemoration of new Russian wonder-workers originated in the sixteenth century after the glorification

13. Mateos, *Typicon*, vol. 2, 144–47.

14. Getcha, *Typicon Decoded*, provides theological reasons for the commemoration of the saints on 280–81.

15. The notion of baptism by blood is most often attributed to St. Cyprian of Carthage. For a summary, see Ferguson, *Baptism in the Early Church*, 360–61.

16. A Monk of the Eastern Church, *Year of Grace*, 218–19.

of several Russian saints at the Moscow councils of 1547 and 1549.[17] The service was not published in the synodal liturgical books and survived primarily in the manuscripts of Old Believers.[18] The Moscow council of 1917–18 considered the proposal of restoring the annual commemoration of all saints of Russia and authorized its annual celebration on the first Sunday of the apostles' fast.[19] The council directed the publication of the service at the end of the Pentecostarion, which places it after the Sunday of All Saints. Nikolai Balashov notes the context of the conciliar consideration of the feast.[20] The council heard and considered the proposal on August 20, 1918, when contemporary martyrdom was a reality for the Russian Orthodox Church. The decision to restore the feast as an annual commemoration illustrated the Church's sense of communion with the saints and their desire to imitate saintly lives during a time of violent civil war.

The commemoration of all saints of Russia, or any national church, has even more narrowly defined local parallels. The Russian and Ukrainian traditions include the appointment of annual commemorations for the saints of Vladimir (June 23), Kyiv (July 15), Moscow (Sunday before August 26), and many other prestigious cities and communities. There are also annual commemorations of the saints of Moldova (October 1) and Belarus (third Sunday after Pentecost).

The local commemorations communicate significant stories that fuse the Orthodox faith with national identity. The liturgical commemoration of saints has the dual function of proclaiming the narrative of the saint's life in thanksgiving to God while simultaneously catechizing the faithful on the life of the saint through abridged versions of the hagiographical narratives. The annual commemoration of saints or a saint display a delicate cross pollination of hagiography, hymnography, and iconography. This tradition is well established in Orthodox Church history from the creation of the synaxarion of the Great Church of Constantinople to the interplay of liturgy and hagiography in the feast of St. Volodymyr.[21]

The hymns from these feasts of saints essentially deliver the primary features of the hagiographical detail in text, image, and sound. Theologically, the hymns embellish the significance of the saint and—occasionally—make

17. Lukashevich, "всех святых, в земле российской просиявщих, неделя."
18. Lukashevich, "всех святых, в земле российской просиявщих, неделя."
19. Destivelle, *Moscow Council,* 311.
20. Balashov, *На пути к,* 427–30.
21. Efthymiadis, *Hagiography,* 129–30.

bold tropological statements designed for the conversion or repentance of people within and outside of the church.

In his study of the reciprocity of hagiography and liturgy in the lives of the saints of early Rus', Sean Griffin succinctly states that liturgical rites and texts inspired the hagiographers who wrote accounts of saints and their accomplishments. The accounts appear in abridged form in the church's hymnographical corpus. Griffin aptly refers to the ongoing cycle of influence as a "liturgical-historiographical-liturgical loop."[22] This is a matter of sources of related fields influencing one another. A liturgical minister reads a hagiographical narrative and incorporates a selection of themes into liturgical hymns. This is a creative process, so the hagiographical text tends to influence the liturgical without necessarily being copied altogether. While attending the service, an attentive scribe edits an existing narrative on the basis of the liturgical text. Griffin's plausible scenario provides an example of the cross-pollination between hagiography and liturgy. Several examples illustrate this point and illuminate the liturgical meaning of feasts of saints.

The Manifold Themes and Functions of Hymnography

Earlier chapters of this study showed how appointed hymns of the feast express its liturgical theology. The hymns appointed to the lives of saints illuminate the macro-level historical context of the local church by referencing places, events, conflicts, and teachings. They enhance the figure's sanctity by comparing them to an archetypal saint, like an apostle.

The troparion for the feast of St. Volodymyr exhibits many of these features. St. Volodymyr was the grand prince of Kyiv, and his place in Orthodox Church history is attributable to his decision to adopt Greek Orthodox Christianity for the people of Rus' in the year 988 CE. A troparion is essentially the primary hymn in the collection of songs for a saint or feast, defining the main themes and summarizing events concisely. Here is the entire text of the troparion for St. Volodymyr, which is Griffin's translation of a fourteenth-century manuscript:[23]

---

22. Griffin, *Liturgical Past*, 239.

23. Griffin, *Liturgical Past*, 235. Griffin takes the troparion from the earliest surviving liturgical office, a fourteenth-century manuscript titled *RNB Sof. 382*. As is the case with many liturgical texts, multiple versions of the troparion are published in service books.

You were like a merchant seeking a fine pearl, O glorious sovereign Vladimir. Sitting on the throne of the divinely saved Kiev, the mother of cities, you tested [the faiths] and sent envoys to the Imperial City to behold the orthodox faith. You thereby found Christ, the priceless pearl, who chose you as a second Paul, and washed away your spiritual and physical blindness in the holy font. We your people therefore celebrate your falling asleep. Pray that the leaders of Rus', the Christ-loving princes, may be saved, together with the multitude entrusted to them.

This unusually long troparion summarizes history and identifies the primary features of Volodymyr's sanctity. The hymn refers to Volodymyr's emissaries, who considered Judaism, Islam, and the Roman Catholic Church before their extraordinary experience in Constantinople. The explicit mentioning of the city of Kyiv demonstrates the local quality of the saint. It also carries a significant theological undertone: each local church bears the fullness of the holiness of the Catholic Church. The hymnographer depicts Volodymyr as someone on a treasure hunt who discovers the most precious bounty of all—Jesus Christ. Interestingly, this particular hymn does not refer to Volodymyr's decision to baptize the population of Kyiv in the faith. Instead, Volodymyr is exulted for his decision to receive baptism.

The hymn calls attention to the stature of Volodymyr's sanctity by aligning him with an archetype—the holy apostle Paul. Paul stopped persecuting the church and became an apostle when he encountered Jesus himself (Acts 9). Paul's encounter with Jesus blinds him, and his sight is restored only after he receives the laying on of hands and baptism (Acts 9:17–18). The liturgical hymnographer compares Volodymyr with Paul. Like Paul, Volodymyr's pre-baptismal life was alien to Christianity. Having encountered Christ through the report of his emissaries, Volodymyr received baptism and, in the process, was healed of his own form of blindness. The literary method also explains Volodymyr's prestigious categorization as a saint who is "equal to the apostles." Again, it is noteworthy that the hymn praises Volodymyr for his own decision to convert through baptism.

The hymns also align Volodymyr with a saint more like him: Constantine. The first hymn of the Vigil intercalated into the verses of Psalm 140 (141) ("Lord, I have cried") states: "you were a second Constantine in word and in deed," comparing Volodymyr's conversion to that of the fourth-century Roman emperor and conqueror.[24] The short hymn on the third ode

24. Translated from Church Slavonic ("Вторый ты был еси Константин") published at http://svhram.info/index.php/o-khrame/nebesnyj-pokrovitel/item/16-служба

of the festal canon (sung at Matins) identifies Volodymyr as an "imitator" of Constantine, who also taught the faith to the people of Rus.[25]

It is essential to emphasize that the hymns are hortatory; they call upon the faithful to pray to the saint and to imitate them, and they entreat the saint to intercede on their behalf. They are not limited to proclaiming selections of the hagiographical narrative. The historical references and comparisons with similar figures are significant aspects of the liturgical function, however. This is a matter of recreating the sacred topography of the saint in the present and using the narrative for the conversion and continued repentance and Christian transformation of the community.

Holiness in Interreligious Conflict

Liturgical commemorations of saints in Orthodoxy often bear the legacy of interreligious conflict. The hymns proclaim tales of theological controversies and church schisms. For example, the commemoration of St. Gregory Palamas on the second Sunday of Lent contains several references to the debate with Catholic theologians on the divine presence in God's essence and energies.

The defense of Orthodoxy from Catholic proselytism appears in the annual commemoration of St. Job of Pochaiv. St. Job's life spanned the end of the sixteenth century through the mid-seventeenth century during the period of the union of Brest and the rebuilding of Orthodox life among Orthodox Ruthenians in the Polish kingdom. The hymns narrating the life of St. Job follow the customary pattern for sanctoral commemorations. They identify his ascetical practices, ceaseless prayer, and defense of Orthodoxy as features manifesting his sanctity.

The hymns of the aposticha at Great Vespers reveal the local dimension of St. Job's life, referring to him as "adornment of the land of Volhynia" and the "star which proceeded from the land of Galicia to the east."[26] A troparion on the fourth ode of the canon at Matins implicitly references the struggle with the Roman Church, calling upon the faithful to praise St. Job for withstanding the "heretics" and for his "zeal for Orthodoxy."[27] The Akathist service mentions St. Job's devotion to a culture

-святому-князюю-владимиру.

25. See Griffin, *Liturgical Past*, 236, for his translation of the Slavonic text.

26. Lambertsen, *Saint Job*, 68.

27. Lambertsen, *Saint Job*, 75.

of education, praising him for his own writings and for his establishment of a monastery printing press.[28]

Two other features are relevant to this matter. The hymns praise St. Job for his devotion to monastic labor, as he himself worked in the garden planting, cultivating, and digging (Ikos 5).[29] Job is also praised for his attendance at the council in Kyiv in 1628, which confirmed the loyalty of bishops and abbots to the Orthodox Church.[30]

St. Job's creation of a printing press at the monastery and attendance at the council are historically significant. References to these events in the festal hymns orient the liturgical participants to the context of the saint's life. These specific references represent the rebuilding of the Orthodox Church in Ruthenian Poland following the union of Brest. Prince Konstantin of Ostrih was one of the first and most influential patrons of education in the general region, establishing an academy with a curriculum on the same level as the Jesuit models of the time.[31] The services of St. Job, then, represent a phase of Orthodox liturgical development that illuminates historical episodes of church schism and conflict. What's more significant for our purposes is that the church willfully expresses its opinion on these matters in the liturgical celebration. Hymns that express the opinions of others, including neighbors of a different Christian tradition, can be problematic for both the Orthodox and people of other faiths.

St. John Maximovich of Shanghai and San Francisco

The services of St. Job mentioned above represent the blueprint for the collection of themes expressed by Orthodox saintly commemoration. The life of a saint of the modern era, John Maximovich, further illustrates these points. St. John Maximovich is unique because he cannot be conveniently categorized as a local saint, since he was the pastor of churches in Harbin, Shanghai, Western Europe, and San Francisco.

In many ways, the services to St. John follow the established sanctoral blueprint. Numerous eyewitnesses testified to St. John's multidimensional life of sanctity. He was an ascetic, a healer, and a shepherd, and the

28. Lambertsen, *Saint Job*, 84.

29. Lambertsen, *Saint Job*, 87.

30. Lambertsen, *Saint Job*, 86. The Akathist mentions Job's attendance at the "sacred council of the Orthodox" in the "divinely saved city" of Kyiv in Kontakion 4.

31. Subtelny, *Ukraine*, 96–99.

services refer to multiple instances of his life. A hymn at Great Vespers captures his journey as the pastor of migrants, referring to him as "the luminary of the Russian diaspora, the teacher of diverse nations, the sojourner amid this transitory world."[32]

St. John's ministry presents a different angle on the relations between Eastern and Western Christians. He restored the annual commemoration of a number of pre-schism saints during his tenure in Western Europe, an act acknowledged by the service.[33] Ikos 7 of the "Akathist Hymn" places St. John in the company of these Western saints, referring to him as a "new" Martin, Germanus, and Hilary, among others.[34] The service contains references to St. John's particular ministry to the Russian diaspora by mentioning Bolshevik persecution of the church and the saint's advocacy of Russia's tsarist legacy. None of the hymns explicitly mention communists or Bolsheviks, but the word "godless" appears in the context of a Christian struggle.[35]

Themes of patronage of Orthodox monarchies appear in the Ikos on the Kontakion and a troparion on ode 8 of the canon. The Ikos expresses a cosmic encomium of St. John and claims that "holy kings honor an advocate for the restoration of Orthodox kingship."[36] The canon troparion acknowledges the collapse of Orthodox monarchies and St. John's steadfast prayer that right-believing kings would receive victory.[37]

In summary, the service to St. John proclaims a narrative of his life and its journey. The hymnographers wrote carefully and emphasized St. John's sanctity instead of using the liturgy to make bold ideological statements. Careful readers and attentive hearers are capable of absorbing the church's opinion on select issues that the hymns express implicitly. These include the church's response to the Bolshevik assault, the notion of divinely appointed kingship in Orthodoxy, and the people's moral failures during tests of faith. The service to St. John is similar to the ones of St. Gregory Palamas

---

32. *Service and Akathist*, 7.

33. "O excellent lover of the glory of the ancient saints unknown to the East and neglected in the West," sessional hymn of Matins, *Service and Akathist*, 18.

34. *Service and Akathist*, 37–38.

35. See, for example, "conflict [which] arose with the godless" in the second hymn on the Praises in *Service and Akathist*, 28.

36. *Service and Akathist*, 24–25.

37. *Service and Akathist*, 26.

and St. Job in the inclusion of references to ideas that are not necessarily essential to the faith, even if the endorsement is implicit.

St. Andrei Şaguna of Transylvania: Orthodoxy and Modern Romania

Our final example of a saint who was a proponent of Orthodoxy and nation building comes from nineteenth-century Romania: Andrei Şaguna, who was a metropolitan of Sibiu. Şaguna's ministry took place during the period of Romanian nation building. Romania became an independent nation-state in 1877, and the Romanian Church declared its autocephaly in 1872 (recognized by the Ecumenical Patriarchate of Constantinople in 1885).[38] The metropolitanate of Sibiu remained within the borders of the Austro-Hungarian Empire during this period. The Orthodox people of Transylvania, Bukovina, and Bessarabia joined the autocephalous Romanian Church in 1918, following the fall of the Habsburg Empire.[39] Şaguna played an important role in emancipating his metropolitanate from Serbian jurisdiction, establishing good relations with the neighboring Uniate Church and advocating for the autonomy of the church from imperial control.[40]

Cyril Hovorun asserts that Şaguna contributed to the creation of a Romanian civil religion during this period together with the Greek Catholic bishop Inokentiu Micu-Klein.[41] Historical evidence demonstrates Şaguna's activities in his metropolitanate and Romanian politics. For our purposes, the hymns written for the service to St. Andrei celebrate both his ecclesial and political accomplishments.[42] For example, one of the hymns, based on Psalm 140, at Little Vespers praises St. Andrei for contributing to the resurrection of the Romanian people and their triumph over the oppressors.[43] In fact, there are numerous references to the oppressors in the hymns of his feast. The hymns of the services mention St. Andrei's accomplishments as a pastor, including the independence of the Transylvanian metropolitanate,

---

38. Mureşan, "Romanian Tradition," 149–50.

39. Mureşan, "Romanian Tradition," 150.

40. Mureşan, "Romanian Tradition," 150.

41. Hovorun, *Political Orthodoxies*, 58–59.

42. For the text of the service, see "Slujba Sfantului Andrei Saguna."

43. "Slujba Sfantului Andrei Saguna."

and the instructions of the ordinances. The fusion of church renewal with the liberation of the Romanian people is a recurring theme of the service.[44]

St. Andrei Şaguna lived during a time of change. The church remembers him for his wise oversight and advocacy of the entire population. The liturgical rites commemorating him illustrate the church's incorporation of national liberation into the ecclesial narrative. Essentially, the church communicates the idea that representing the people in the political arena is a holy deed. Scholars should take note of the political theology communicated by the rite—there is no hesitation to praise a saint who contributed to the liberation of a nation from imperial oppression.

Orthodox Idea Feasts?

Most of the examples cited in this chapter draw from the Russian and Ukrainian traditions. The commemorations illustrate how the festal hymnography identifies saintly acts that manifest the figure's holiness. Each example reveals the work of the saint for a particular community. St. Volodymyr's ministry was for the people of the "divinely saved" Kyiv. St. Job shepherded the Orthodox communities of Galicia and Volyn'. St. John ministered to several communities in Harbin, Shanghai, Western Europe, and San Francisco. The connection of a saint to ministry in a particular city is a hallmark feature of the Orthodox liturgical year with seemingly countless examples.

The Baptism of Rus' as an Idea Feast

The next example brings us to St. Volodymyr once again but for a different occasion—the Baptism of Rus' on July 28. This feast is significant for two reasons. First, it is a celebration of the baptism of a nation. Second, the meaning of the feast evolves in real time in response to new geopolitical conditions.

The hymns appointed to the feast call both the church and the nation to rejoice and speak of the unity of Christ with the Church of Rus'

---

44. See, for example, the kathisma (*sedealna*) hymn at Matins, which praises Andrei for announcing the deliverance of the Romanian nation and therefore giving hope to believers: "Pe arhipastorul cel luminat al Transilvaniei, pe Sfantul Andrei, dupa vrednicie sa-l cinstim, cel ce, ca un luceafar prealuminos, a rasarit sa vesteasca zorile izbavirii neamului romanesc" ("Slujba Sfantului Andrei Saguna").

through marital imagery. The first hymn appointed to Psalm 140 (141) of Vespers speaks of Christ as the bride betrothing the Church of Rus' to himself. The second and third hymns exhort the land of Rus' to rejoice on the occasion of receiving baptism in Christ, along with the blessing of deliverance from ignorance and heresy.

These appeals to both the land and the Church of Rus' occur repeatedly throughout the text, and they include many references to Volodymyr, Olga, and the degree of transformation that occurred in Rus' following the decision to convert to Christianity. In a certain sense, the celebration seems to fit the pattern of a local church celebration, since each city has its collection of beloved saints. A hymn appointed to the praises at Matins reveals the unique feature of the Baptism of Rus.' It recounts the saints who labored in various regions: the apostles in Jerusalem, Peter and Paul in Rome, Thomas in India, and Mark in Egypt. The text expresses thanks for the first apostolic preaching in Rus' by St. Andrew and the act of baptism by St. Volodymyr, who is—again—compared with Constantine.

Originally, Rus' was not one united imperial state but rather a loose confederation of peoples rooted in strong cities.[45] The texts examined here mention Kyiv most frequently, but Novgorod and Vladimir-Suzdal were also strong centers with autonomous local traditions. Kyiv was the most prestigious center, so much that the church's primate retained the title of metropolitan of Kyiv long after the city was sacked and ruined in 1240 CE, and the primary cell migrated north to Moscow. Kyiv eventually became the primary see for the minority Orthodox Ruthenian population under Poland, while Moscow's stature increased when the patriarchate of Constantinople elevated it to the status of patriarchate in 1589 CE. The relationship between Kyiv and Moscow took many twists and turns from the seventeenth century until now. The point is that Kyiv was no longer the seat of ecclesial authority of the Orthodox descendants of the city-states of Rus.' Moscow seized control of that authority until Kyiv began to assert its independence again in the twentieth and twenty-first centuries.

---

45. Serhii Plokhy argues that Kyivan princes adjusted their loyalties from the entire realm of Kyivan Rus' to peripheral principalities that were able to rival Kyiv by the twelfth and thirteenth centuries. He identifies Vladimir-Suzdal as Russia's forerunner, Polotsk as Belarus's, and Galicia-Volhynia as the original cell of Ukrainian nation-building. See Plokhy, *Gates of Europe*, 48. For a deeper dive into this important issue, see the analysis of the early stages of a scholarly debate on the legacy of Kyivan Rus' in Plokhy, *Unmaking Imperial Russia*, 134–52.

The liturgical hymns for the Baptism of Rus' do not mention Moscow, however. Nor do they mention Russia, Ukraine, or Belarus, the three primary nations descendant of the medieval city-states. The hymns themselves mention Kyiv and Rus'. The variants of these texts are relevant. For example, at least one Ukrainian translation of the text changes Rus' to Kyivan Rus' and refers to the Kyivan Church instead of the Church of Rus'. This particular translation and redaction of the liturgical text emphasizes the unicity of the Kyivan Church. The ambiguity of the translation makes it difficult to argue that the original church that embraced Christianity under St. Volodymyr could be subordinate to the Moscow Patriarchate.

The English translation of the texts used by the Russian Orthodox Church outside of Russia (ROCOR) are also insightful.[46] The texts consistently translate *"zemle russkaia"* into "Russian land" and *"tserkov russkuiu"* into Russian Church. The church's Slavonic text suggests Rus' instead of Russia.

The appearance of new texts and variant translations points to a historical problem. The churches celebrating the feast of the Baptism of Rus'—primarily those of Russia, Ukraine, and Belarus—are no longer united politically. Each has a legitimate claim as descendants and heirs of the original Church of Rus'. The current independence of the nations and their churches places stress on the community's celebration of the event because of the break with the past. This is particularly problematic for Russia and Ukraine, as they have been at war since 2014. The use of Kyivan Rus' and the Kyivan Church suggests exclusivity for Ukraine, since Kyiv is its capital. The translations of "Russian land" and "Russian Church" suggest exclusivity for Russia. The celebrations of the Baptism of Rus' have become contested interpretive spaces, especially in Ukraine.

The feast of the Baptism of Rus' on July 28 became quite prominent in 1988, when the Orthodox Church celebrated the millennium of this historical event. At the time, the primary celebration occurred in Moscow, as it was the seat of the Soviet Union. In successive years, large public celebrations have occurred throughout Ukraine. In 2008, President Victor Yushchenko organized a major state celebration and invited Patriarch Bartholomew of Constantinople to preside on the 1020th anniversary. The

46. Here are the two ROCOR publications: https://ru.eadiocese.org/files/resources/liturgical/services/Baptism-of-Rus-SL.pdf (Church Slavonic) and https://ru.eadiocese.org/files/resources/liturgical/services/Baptism-of-Rus-EN.pdf (English translation). A Ukrainian translation of the text (OCU?) can be found here: http://kyiv-pravosl.info/2014/07/26/sluzhba-svyatu-hreschennya-kyjivskoji-rusi/.

patriarch was invited under the pretext of uniting the divided churches in Ukraine and granting formal autocephaly (ecclesial independence) to the new church. When the proposed plan did not come to pass, one of the Ukrainian churches had its own celebration. The churches assembled in public spaces of symbolic significance to stake their claim as the legitimate heirs of the Church of Rus' and Volodymyr's baptism. This is now an annual event with competing public processions of the cross. In Ukraine, the churches gather separately at the monument to St. Volodymyr for enormous public liturgies. They make grandiose claims about the numbers of faithful who participated in processions, sometimes up to 350,000, to show their preeminence.[47] These claims essentially say that size matters—the larger procession belongs to the legitimate heir of the church and people of Rus'. The Russian Orthodox Church used one of these anniversaries to organize a stational celebration in three cities—Moscow, Kyiv, and Minsk. This celebration, in 2013, was designed to show that the three contemporary descendants of Rus'—Russia, Ukraine, and Belarus—were united as one Church of Rus' under the Moscow Patriarchate.[48]

47. See the public comments by the Metropolitan Antony of the Ukrainian Orthodox Church (under Moscow) on July 27, 2021: Керуючий справами УПЦ підбив підсумки Великого Хресного ходу з нагоди 1033-річчя Хрещення Русі (The head of church affairs of the UOC summarized the great cross procession on the occasion of the 1033rd anniversary of the Baptism of Rus'), https://news.church.ua/2021/07/27/keruyuchij-spravami-upc-pidbiv-pidsumki-velikogo-xresnogo-xodu-z-nagodi-1033-richchya-xreshhennya-rusi/.

48. Denysenko, "Chaos in Ukraine," 242–59.

Hermeneutical Questions in Sanctoral Commemorations

The examples cited in this section present hermeneutical problems of saintly commemorations. It is entirely possible for memories of the past to go unnoticed. To my knowledge, only fellow scholars are paying scrupulous attention to references to Latin heretics on the Sunday of St. Gregory Palamas or in the services to St. Job of Pochaiv or St. John. The church's pointed recollection of past events has the potential to create hermeneutical problems, however. Many ordinary people have noticed anti-Semitic tropes in the services of Holy Week, and some scholars have suggested removing those passages or composing new hymns.[49] The references to St. John's advocacy for the restoration of an Orthodox monarchy could be upsetting to people who view Orthodoxy as compatible with other forms of government.

In the case of the Baptism of Rus', it has become an occasion to stake a strong claim for exclusive legitimacy. Some politicians have used the notion of a united medieval Rus', anchored by the liturgical event, to advocate for the reunification of its contemporary descendants. Currently, the public liturgy celebrating this feast has instead become a spectacle, and this is because politicians have transformed the anniversary of a historical event into an opportunity to promote an idea.

The current manipulation of the feast of the Baptism of Rus' by politicians is an exception to the liturgical norm of sanctoral commemorations. By and large, feasts of saints provide an opportunity for each community to adopt any number of saints venerated by the universal church. The example of St. Jon Maximovich is relevant here. The Holy Virgin Cathedral in San Francisco is the site of St. John's shrine and the primary location of his veneration. The cathedral welcomes visitors and pilgrims of all backgrounds who come to the shrine to beseech St. John's intercession. St. John's ministry extends far beyond the walls of the Holy Virgin Cathedral. A number of Orthodox churches include him in their annual celebrations, possess his relics and icon, and commemorate him on his appointed feast. Again, the universal adoption of a local saint brings the sacred topography of the saint into the community seeking their patronage.

The commemoration of saints also has a strong catechetical character. The festal hymns proclaim a synthesized narrative of the saint's life. The faithful's hearing of the narrative grants them access to church history and, more importantly, invites them to commune with the saint, adopting them as their patron and seeking to imitate their sanctity. The power of sanctoral narrative follows an oral tradition passed on from Jews to Christians, and it continues to have the capacity to shape and form the faithful today.

That said, the examples cited here clearly demonstrate that the church presents its own perspective. One cannot claim that this viewpoint is historically precise and objective. The authors of hagiographical accounts and hymns are human beings with opinions. In some instances, the liturgical participant may need assistance in navigating the interpretive space of

---

49. Groen, "Anti-Judaism," 369–87.

sanctoral commemorations. We will return to this issue in our remarks about problems and possibilities for the liturgical year.

Feasts of Icons

This study has presented the appearance of Marian and sanctoral feasts on the calendar of the Orthodox liturgical year. Sacred topography had a crucial function in the origins of many feasts. The distribution of relics made it possible for other Christian communities to adopt the commemoration. In the Byzantine tradition, the tone for installing relics and creating shrines of saints in sister churches was set in the Blachernai and Chalkoprateia churches in Constantinople.[50] Daniel Galadza notes that the installation of the Marian relics in these churches enhanced Constantinople's identity as a holy city.[51] The pattern of expanding sacred topography, enabled by the transfer of relics, paved a path for new Marian and sanctoral appearances and events, especially through icons.

A significant aspect of this development was Mary's assumption of the role of queen and protectress of the imperial capital. Her miraculous defense of Constantinople during the Avar Siege of 626 CE became a central feature of the empire's historical memory and her continued role as the city's patron, as described by Bissera Pentcheva.[52] Pentcheva notes that eyewitnesses described Mary as fighting the enemies while walking on the city walls.[53] In this sense, Mary inherited the protective function exercised previously by pagan goddesses of war.[54]

The development of a popular cult in the city, namely the Blachernai Monastery, established a location of popular Marian piety that became inscribed on Orthodox Marian piety through the modern period.[55] Pentcheva notes that the monastery sustained Mary's identity as victor and guardian on the basis of the Avar Siege account.[56] This account became a blueprint for new Marian apparitions in Orthodox history, many of which populate the liturgical calendar and are observed by communities.

50. See Fassler, "First Marian Feast," 46–47.

51. Galadza, *Liturgy and Byzantinization*, 249.

52. Pentcheva, *Icons and Power*, 37–59. See also 22–23.

53. Pentcheva, *Icons and Power*, 38.

54. Pentcheva, *Icons and Power*, 38.

55. Pentcheva, *Icons and Power*, 62–63.

56. Pentcheva, *Icons and Power*, 62.

Liturgy and church architecture experienced a metamorphosis in the wake of the iconoclastic controversy of the eighth and ninth centuries. A typical middle-Byzantine structure accommodated iconographic programs, appointing Christ Pantocrator to the dome above the nave and Mary Theotokos to the apse of the sanctuary.[57] The decrees of the seventh ecumenical council (787 CE) called for the veneration of icons in churches, private homes, and in the public spaces. This development was essentially a new branch in the tree of liturgical development, related to the power of relics in influencing liturgical practice and expanding sacred topography.

Marian icons were particularly powerful in the consciousness of the official church and in popular piety. The famous Virgin Hodegetria icon was eventually housed at the Hodegon Monastery in Constantinople and was carried in procession through the city each Tuesday in the late-Byzantine period.[58] The Hodegetria icon functioned as a blueprint for derivative Marian icons, such as the Virgin Eleusa. Its popularity made it the most widely copied Marian icon. The Byzantines fused their identification of Mary as the protectress of the capital and defender of the empire with rite by carrying the icon to the city walls to protect soldiers and citizens. Instances of public processions in search of Marian intervention for miraculous healings and protection from adversaries became entrenched in Byzantine religious culture. Orthodox Christians believe that Mary responded favorably to the petitions of the church and intervened through appearances and miracles worked through her icons. Such appearances constituted new events that were annually commemorated in the liturgical year.

The church has many Marian feasts inspired by wonder-working icons, including some now commemorated by Orthodox Christians in the West. These include the aforementioned Hodegetria Icon Feast (June 20), Vladimir Mother of God (August 26, June 23, May 21), the Virgin Kykkou of Cyprus, and the Hawaii Iveron Icon, among many others.

One common element shared by many of the icon feasts is the attribution of authorship to the evangelist Luke. Church tradition held that Luke painted the Hodegetria and Vladimir Mother of God icons.[59] The attribution of authorship of the Hodegetria to Luke is extant in the twelfth

---

57. Grishin, "Eastern Orthodox Iconography," 373–74; Schulz, *Byzantine Liturgy*, 50–62.

58. Patterson Ševčenko, "Virgin Hodegetria," 2172.

59. See Patterson Ševčenko, "Virgin Hodegetria," 2172; Ouspensky and Lossky, *Meaning of Icons*, 96.

century. The Vladimir icon arrived in Vladimir from Constantinople via Kyiv.[60] Ouspensky and Lossky observe that the three commemorations of the icon are inspired by divine aid in Moscow's defeat of Tatar assaults.[61] Mary's defense of Orthodox people in warfare is a common theme of festal icon commemorations.

The processes guiding icons to annual commemoration on the liturgical calendar were complex and involved many parties. Vera Shevzov demonstrates how ordinary people came to venerate established icons and how lay reports of miraculous interventions and appearances were received by church authorities. Shevzov writes that the distribution of copies of famous icons stimulated veneration of the icon by a larger segment of the Orthodox population.[62] One person's experience of a native icon of Greece resulted in an update of the icon's story, making it more "relevant" to the community venerating a copy.[63]

Shevzov's rigorous exploration of primary sources yields examples of local icon veneration in which laity witnessed epiphanies and requested synodal blessing for the veneration of the icons.[64] One of the examples concerned a peasant who observed several icons of the Mother of God "Multiplier of Grains" in village churches and chapels. The Holy Synod denied the petition of the peasant and the cosigners despite his testimony of miraculous epiphanies.[65] Shevzov observes that church authorities were anxious about confirming an icon that had no known stylistic antecedent. She also suggests that the official denials reveal different concepts about church authority and the people's sense of religious experience and meaning.[66]

Shevzov's differentiation of officially sanctioned icon veneration and popular traditions of icons that are never entered into the calendar evokes a well-known reality about the glorification of saints. Some communities venerate saints and create rites celebrating their lives before the church officially recognizes them and blesses the composition of an official narrative.[67] In other words, Orthodox tradition continues to venerate saints

60. Ouspensky and Lossky, *Meaning of Icons*, 96.

61. Ouspensky and Lossky, *Meaning of Icons*, 96n2.

62. Shevzov, "Miracle-working Icons," 34–35.

63. Shevzov, "Miracle-working Icons," 34.

64. Shevzov, "Petitions," 229–48.

65. Shevzov, "Petitions," 243, 247.

66. Shevzov, "Petitions," 231.

67. On this matter, see Michael Plekon's commentary on the "new" hagiography in

ritually without official additions to the liturgical year. Shevzov's argument about religious authority confirms our earlier observation about the church expressing its unique viewpoint in hagiographical narratives and hymnography. Religious officials seek to control the process by asserting their authority in blessing or denying permission to venerate saints and icon feasts. This exercise of control raises questions on the interpretive space of festal commemorations of icons and relics.

One final aspect of icon feasts serves a brief commentary. They are extraordinarily popular in contemporary church life. Famous wonder-working icons and relics often go on tour, with visitations organized for multiple parishes of a given city or diocese. Orthodox people and pilgrims are invited to attend divine services to venerate the icon. It is customary for the host church to publish and distribute copies of the icons to participants. Seeking miraculous healing or conceptions are among the motivations bringing ordinary people to the church for venerating a wonder-working icon.

In one fairly recent episode (2011), the relic of Mary's belt, currently housed at the Vatopedi Monastery on Mount Athos, went on a visitation to Moscow.[68] Thousands of Muscovites and pilgrims stood in a cold November line to venerate it, and many of them came in search of a miracle. Church authorities made copies of the belt, distributed them, and seized the occasion to evangelize the general public—in some cases, through stories of miraculous healings that took place through Mary's intercession. This episode went viral in mainstream media because of the sheer number of pilgrims who attended the event, but it is not uncommon, as Orthodox throughout the world continue to organize and make pilgrimages in search of healing and mercy.

The phenomenon itself raises ethical questions about the narrative that develops around such visitations. On the one hand, Orthodox liturgical theology confesses divine action, the descent of the Spirit and the outpouring of God's divine grace upon people when they gather and make their petitions. This liturgical theology follows the classical dynamic of anamnesis and epiclesis. The church petitions with the confidence that God will respond today on the basis of the past; in epiclesis, God is present.

Plekon, *Hidden Holiness*, 29–40.

[68] See Wortley, "Marian Relics," 181–87; Shevzov, "Women on the Fault," 125; Denysenko, "An Appeal to Mary," 1061–92.

On the other hand, appealing to the fundamental human need for good health and desire for fertility by making implicit promises that Mary might perform a miracle seems disingenuous at best and sinful at worst. Once again, the issue at hand is the interpretive space of the liturgical occasion and the limits on claims church officials can make.

The ethics of the agency of icons took a dark turn in Russia's invasion of Ukraine that began in February 2022. On March 13, 2022, the Sunday of Orthodoxy, Patriarch Kirill (Gundyev) of the Russian Orthodox Church gave the Our Lady of Augustow icon to Victor Zolotov, the leader of Russia's National Guard.[69] This Marian icon depicts Mary's appearance to Russian soldiers during World War I. Zolotov asserted his confidence that Mary would lead Russia to victory over the Ukrainian "Nazis," a gross politicization of the liturgical use of icons. This was the recent and perhaps most controversial episode in the manipulation of the meaning of icons in modern Orthodox history.

The Liturgical Year at Home

Special ritual traditions mark the intersection of the church's official observance of the liturgical year with significant domestic rites. In earlier chapters, we have introduced the practices of a collection of blessings associated with feasts of the liturgical year. The church blesses homes throughout the season following the Theophany feast, blessed candles on Hypapante, fruit on the Transfiguration, and flowers on the Dormition. Some traditions belong to specific cultures, such as the Serbian *Krsn Slava* and the Greek tradition *Vasilopita* (savory bread on St. Basil's Day). The solemn blessing of meats, cheeses, and other savory foods in the Pascha basket is a staple of many Slavic Orthodox and Greek Catholic communities. Each of these blessings is an intersection of the church's official liturgy with people in their homes.

The last section of this chapter briefly describes three of these events: the tradition of the Serbian *Krsna Slava*, the *Vasilopita* bread on January 1, and the *Sviata Vechera* (Holy Supper) observed on Christmas Eve among Ukrainian, Slovak, and Romanian Orthodox and Greek Catholics.

---

69. *The Times*, "Times View on the Russian Patriarch's Backing."

Krsna Slava: Patron Saints and Families

The *Krsna Slava* is a Serbian tradition wherein the family adopts a patron saint.[70] It originated either as a Christianized pagan ritual or as a Christian evangelical response to pagan rituals and traditions. The *Slava* is a family rite that begins in the church and migrates to the family home. It requires food—boiled wheat (koljivo), a special cake or bread, red wine, oil, and incense. The priest presides at the *Slava*, offers the cake and wheat to God, cuts the cake in the form of a cross and pours red wine on it. The ritual signifies the family's participation in Christ's suffering and entreaty for the forgiveness of the family's sins. The domestic aspect of the *Slava* continues at home in the form of a family feast, which includes appointed foods and a toast offered in honor of God and the patron saint.

The *Slava* is significant for a number of reasons. First, it is customary for Orthodox and other Christians throughout the world to celebrate the day of their patron saint. The Serbian celebration is an enhancement of the typical saint's day celebration. It is a hereditary, family feast. The family dimension distinguishes the *Slava* from a more typical celebration of an annual saint or name's day. The saint becomes the patron of the household and remains the family's saint, since the *Slava* passes down from father to son.[71] The household rite magnifies the communal quality of such rituals, as the household celebration includes multiple people.

This unique Serbian family ritual is yet another confirmation of the power of the cult of the saints. But there is much more going on here that needs to be discussed. First, the *Slava* demonstrates an organic relationship between the domestic household and the church. The shared ritual space that calls for the migration of the liturgical rite to the home resists any temptation to subordinate domestic rites to the official liturgy of the church. Second, the prominence of food is notable. While most liturgical analysis concentrates on the bread and cup of the Eucharist, the rite itself originated as a shared meal. The offering of wheat, bread, and wine for the *Slava* and the underpinning of offering food and drink for forgiveness and blessing places it in the extended family of meal rites, including the Eucharist and Jewish festival meals. There is no need to categorize the *Slava* as a derivative of or subordinate to the Eucharist; it is another reminder that

70. Hadžibulič, "*Slava* Celebration," 37.

71. Hadžibulič affirms the patrimonial quality of the celebration, as the eldest male traditionally acts as host. She adds that a widow can assume the role of host if she inherits her late husband's *slava* (Hadžibulič, "*Slava* Celebration," 38).

Jews and Christians have always blessed and petitioned God at the table. It is in this sense that one can describe the *Slava* as sacramental, a unique and organic blend of official and domestic liturgy.

Vasilopita: Good Fortune for the New Year and a Cake in Honor of St. Basil

Every year, on or shortly after January 1, Greek Orthodox Christians share a cake baked in honor of St. Basil of Caesarea.[72] The rite of baking, cutting, and distributing the cake, culminating in the discovery of the coin by the most fortunate participant, was originally domestic. It is now customary for parishes to celebrate the rite as communities, beginning with a short prayer service, followed by a ceremonial cutting and distribution of the cake. There are multiple variants of this rite, as some sing the troparion for the feast of Christ's birth, whereas others sing the troparion of St. Basil.

The popular narrative of the *Vasilopita* explains that the pieces of the cake are cut in honor of Christ, Mary, and then St. Basil, in that order.[73] In parishes and homes, the tradition of baking and distributing the *Vasilopita* is attributed to St. Basil himself. According to the story, St. Basil demanded that the emperor repent for placing too heavy a tax burden on the populace of his see in Caesarea of Cappadocia. The emperor handed St. Basil the coins the people had scrounged to pay the tax. St. Basil attempted to return money to the people by placing all of the tax money in one enormous pita and distributing it to them after the Divine Liturgy.[74] In present ritual practice, the one who receives the coin is not only the beneficiary of good fortune for the year, but is also tasked with providing for the poor, widows, and orphans.

Questions on the actual origins of the rite abound. Margaret Hasluck viewed the attribution to St. Basil as dubious. She asserted that parallel domestic rites of baking cakes with coins in honor of kings in the West suggest that the Greek tradition could have originated as a rite of fortune

72. For a detailed description of variant celebrations of the rite and an older commentary on its origins, see Hasluck, "Basil-Cake," 143–77. There are numerous versions of short prayer services for the *Vasilopita* circulating online. See, for example, the bilingual service published online by St. Basil's Greek Orthodox Church in Chicago at https://www.stbasilchicago.org/service-books/.

73. Hasluck mentions some of the variations of the symbolic significance of the pieces of cake in "Basil-Cake," 144–45.

74. The legend claims that St. Basil arrived at this solution following intense prayer.

bestowing honor on the finder of the coin in the name of the king or emperor (*basileus*).[75] It was not uncommon for agrarian rites to acquire new meanings when they became associated with Christian commemorations on the calendar. In this case, a domestic rite of laborers dependent on bountiful harvests was a good candidate for Christianization on the feast of St. Basil. For Greeks and other Byzantine Christians throughout the world, the *Vasilopita* has become an opportunity to fuse the anticipation of joy with the message to distribute alms in a rite that is now both domestic and communal.

Sviata Vechera—The Holy Supper of Christmas Eve

Orthodox, Greek Catholics, and some Roman Catholics of Poland, the Czech Republic, Slovakia, Ukraine, and Belarus observe a rich domestic tradition on Christmas Eve. This tradition is known as *Sviata Vechera*, or Holy Supper. Unlike the *Slava*, the *Sviata Vechera* is a purely domestic rite without an obvious intersection with official liturgy. It is likely that *Sviata Vechera* originated as a pre-Christian agrarian feast that was updated by Christians to express Christian themes.[76] The domestic ritual features a number of specially prepared foods. The twelve dishes originally represented a feast consisting of foods stored for sustenance during the winter. Originally, each food represented one of the twelve months of the year, an interpretation that evolved into dishes honoring the twelve apostles. Boiled wheat (*kutya*), breads, dumplings (*varenyky*), and dried fish were among the foods taken from storage to greet the solstice. There was no need for families to change the appointed foods for the Christian feast, only the themes. Neighbors in the village would greet the host in song and wish him and his family a good harvest and wealth. The Christian adaptation of these carols revised the texts to praise God for the birth of the Incarnate Son but retained numerous verses of goodwill for the host.

    Sviata Vechera is an example of festive fasting, as the Orthodox Church designates Christmas Eve as a strict fast day. Ideally, people would eat minimally, just enough to sustain them through the day until breaking the fast after receiving Holy Communion. The monastic meal is meager and simple, consisting of dried fruits and bread. *Sviata Vechera* exudes the

---

75. Hasluck, "Basil-Cake," 164.

76. I consulted the following sources for this brief description: Antofijchuk, "Різдво Христове"; Forostij, "Від Різдва."

principle of simple food by abstaining from meat and drawing from storage. The meal itself is both ordered and festive. The head of the household acts as a host, welcoming guests and strangers and greeting the newborn Christ with a series of domestic rites.

Sviata Vechera takes place independently of the official liturgical rites and is observed either before or after the Christmas Vigil service. In many contemporary communities, *Sviata Vechera* has expanded beyond the nuclear family and takes place in a parish community setting. It is both similar to and different from the *Krsna Slava*. The genetic code of *Sviata Vechera* is purely domestic, the household celebration of a feast, another instance of an important rite observed by families. Unlike the *Krsna Slava*, the intersection of *Sviata Vechera* with the official liturgy is limited. The two rites share similar themes and are compatible, yet distinct. The resilience of the *Sviata Vechera* tradition is notable. Many families continue to observe it, albeit with local adaptations. Its status as a beloved domestic tradition demonstrates its power among the people.

Conclusion

This chapter explored what I have described as "everything else" in the liturgical year. The rapid spread of the cult of the saints from the second century and beyond highlights the importance of sacred topography and narrative. The ritual telling and retelling of the story of local saints follows the pattern of many religious traditions. The saint becomes the patron of the local community, and the space inhabited by the saint is holy by contact.

The narrative is an equal partner to the saint's holy space in the local community. As people in neighboring communities hear the story of the new saint, they want to adopt them and take on the narrative and physical objects that connote their presence and sanctity. The cult of the saints, then, is like a primary body of water that feeds systems of rivers, streams, and creeks. Entire regions, nations, and continents adopt the saint and recreate the locus of their sacred topography in a new place, among new people.

This chapter also shows that the saint's holy activity is not limited to their primary narrative, place, and annual commemoration. The saint remains active among the people who have adopted them through icons; in the Orthodox tradition, this is particularly true for Marian icon feasts. The new appearances through icons added more commemorations and therefore more icons to the liturgical calendar.

The brief description of feasts representing the intersection of domestic and official liturgical rites reminds us that the domestic table was and remains the original place of festal celebration. In some cases, the domestic intersects strongly with the church's liturgy (*Krsna Slava* and *Vasilopita*), whereas in others, the connection is less obvious (*Sviata Vechera*). The sheer number of examples of domestic rites, whether liturgical or not, yields two observations. The institutional church cannot and should not attempt to control and subordinate domestic celebrations to the official liturgy. God is present everywhere and in all things and comes to God's people wherever they are gathered, at home, in church, and elsewhere. Second, the sustained power of the domestic celebration and its inscription on the liturgical year magnifies a second dimension of divine presence. People seek, praise, petition, and meet God in the most mundane, ordinary activities—eating and drinking. The faithful believe God comes to them at their family celebrations as well as the church's official liturgy.

It is this sustained evidence of people seeking God through everyday rites that raises questions about certain aspects of the liturgical rites. What is the threshold for an icon feast—when does it transition from a commemoration of divine or saintly presence to the church's commodification of relics and miracles? And what of the narratives underpinning certain celebrations—when do they change from stories deepening communion with God to events supporting the church's ideological agenda? We take up these and other questions in the next chapter.

5

Problems, Opportunities, Time

H AVING DESCRIBED THE NUTS and bolts of the Orthodox liturgical year, we now devote our full attention to problems and opportunities. Invoking the possibility of problems suggests that there is something amiss in the entire system of the church year. Some readers might object to the raising of this possibility. A dominant school of Orthodox liturgical thought views the liturgical year as the natural outcome of an organic process of development. Adherents of this school might object to the identification of problems as an act of dishonor or irreverence against the Church's celebration of the life and the presence of Christ, Mary, and the saints.

This study views the liturgy like an attentive gardener. The garden itself is healthy, but only if the gardener cultivates the soil, waters and seeds regularly, removes weeds, and trims shrubs and branches to prevent overgrowth from engulfing the native plants. The Church's appointed role as steward of the liturgy requires attentive gardening. It is irresponsible and unnecessary to remove native and essential plants and shrubs. It is necessary to keep the garden clean to maintain its optimal health.

The plants and shrubs populating the garden of the Orthodox liturgical year are ancient and venerable. Their roots run deep, and they continue to bring forth fruit, thanks to the fertile soil, sun, shade, and water provided by God. As the stewards of the liturgical garden, the Orthodox Church cares for the plants and receives the blessings of life-giving produce. The Church has not always kept the garden tidy, however. There is a great deal of overgrowth, and the plot needs cleaning.

The Church needs to trim some of the overgrowth to restore the optimal balance of sun and shade in the garden. Examples of overgrowth include clusters of services centered around major feasts and the proliferation of saintly celebrations within the liturgical year. A selection of other issues is also worthy of discussion. These include the dissonance between the Lenten preparatory period and Lent, the sheer volume of themes expressed by the liturgical sources, the temptation to exploit certain feasts for ideological purposes, and the question of commodifying liturgy during festal commemorations of relics and icons. In some of these cases, the primary foundation of a festal commemoration provides an opportunity to reclaim or transform the occasion for the benefit of the people. This chapter therefore analyzes both problems and opportunities, sometimes in the same section.

The final issue requiring analysis is time. Theologians tend to describe the liturgical year as a particular concept of time. The commemorations of people and events depend on their historical dating, a process that can be both speculative and precise, depending on the date and its supporting information. Some theologians describe liturgy as an experience of the already but not yet, a foretaste of the kingdom to come, anchored in God's past activity and confident that he will come again. Another school sees time as sanctified by the incarnation of Christ so that historical commemorations of time signify God's deliverance of salvation in some way.

After reviewing a selection of conceptions of time, I will present my own hypothesis. Time is one of numerous aspects of the liturgical year system in Orthodoxy. I argue that the community itself and its tradition of eyewitness accounts to events and people is just as important to the development of liturgical year commemorations as concepts of time.

What Does It Mean to Keep the Feast?

Some of the feasts of the Orthodox tradition are demanding if they are observed without abbreviations and omissions. A complete observation of Christmas would entail the Royal Hours, Vesperal Liturgy on Christmas Eve, Vigil, and Divine Liturgy on the feast, not to mention the related synaxis of the Theotokos on December 26. The services of the Theophany are equal in rigor, a package that includes the synaxis of St. John on January 7 with the addition of the blessing of waters appended to the liturgy.

No cycle is more demanding than Holy Week and Pascha. Those who attend all paschal services find themselves in church for the long Eucharistic Vigil (observed on Holy Saturday), the Nocturne, Matins, and Liturgy of Pascha (before midnight and into the early hours of Sunday), Paschal

Vespers (Sunday afternoon), and Liturgy of Bright Monday or Tuesday (or both). In recent years, a meme has circulated on social media proclaiming "Christ is Risen! And the priest is dead." Clergy and the faithful have reported such sheer exhaustion from Holy Week and Pascha that they struggle to find energy to engage in the post-paschal period, which is teeming with meaning, as we have discussed.[1]

The clusters of services celebrating a feast raise questions about participation. How is one to interpret a sequence of services? Are the services a progression, gradually immersing participants into the festal journey that leads to the Eucharist? Or are they the result of historical amalgamation, leaving the participant free to choose the office that coheres with their daily schedule? What happens if a sequence of services includes two Eucharists? Is the first of those anticipatory, an entrance into the ultimate liturgical completion? How does one evaluate the participant's engagement in the feast? Is something amiss if they observe only Vespers or Vigil or partake in one of two appointed Eucharists? Is it possible for the Church to move the date of a fixed feast to allow for maximal participation?

I have frequently referred to liturgical expansion in this study to demonstrate how a solemn feast takes on new themes on the days surrounding the core celebration. In this sense, there is nothing wrong with expansion itself; it is indeed the outcome of an organic process of liturgical development. It is reasonable for certain communities of faith to observe the entirety of the cycle of the most rigorous festal services. Monasteries and cathedrals with numerous clergy, singers, and faithful who attend services at different hours and times are able to observe the entire cycle.

The matter becomes more complicated when the church begins to view the most rigorous version of the cycle as normative for the whole Church. The complete observance of Holy Week and Pascha, with limits on abbreviations and omissions, characterizes this perspective. Parishes of all jurisdictions and sizes are expected to observe the complete cycle of services even if this requires one priest and a small group of singers to handle all of the celebration and singing.

The notion of the cycle itself as the festal journey's destiny tends to identify one moment as the highlight. For Holy Week and Pascha, the Midnight Matins and Divine Liturgy is broadly identified as the goal. In plain words—if one is absent from these services, they have not participated in

1. See Denysenko, *People's Faith*, 80–82.

Pascha. The same principle applies to Christmas—if one does not attend the Divine Liturgy on December 25, one has missed Christmas.

Orthodox culture has the same perception of other feasts even if they are less solemn. If one does not attend one of the services appointed to the feast of Christ, Mary, or a major saint that takes place during the week—especially the Divine Liturgy—one has missed out on the feast.

Historically, Orthodoxy has discovered a way to navigate the problem of lax attendance for feasts that fall during the week. Many parishes move the feast to the Sunday after, combining its propers with the cycle of resurrection readings and hymns, so the people experience both the feast and Sunday. The liturgical pattern of the after-feast period promotes this kind of blending, as the festal hymns are added to the Sunday celebration. The leave-taking of a feast takes place on the last day, and the feast is celebrated in its fullness, a repeat of the original rite and propers.

Recognizing that many faithful cannot obtain leave time for a weekday feast, some parishes will celebrate a Vesperal Liturgy on the eve of the feast, so the people can partake of the festal fullness—the Eucharist. This particular perspective on festal periods identifies the Divine Liturgy of the feast as its high point—not to diminish the significance of the Vigil but to refer to the Eucharist as the key moment.

The compromise described in the preceding paragraph does not satisfy all observers. Some remain vehemently opposed to reconfiguring the feast so that people can partake of Communion in a Vesperal Liturgy.[2] Others reject the possibility of moving a feast to the next possible Sunday. The compromise does not apply to the solemn feasts of Christmas, Theophany, and Pascha because of their significance. One does not move Christmas to the nearest Sunday. The matter of multiple services is magnified with these three feasts because many people simply select offices that are most convenient for them. Many people have responsibilities to visit with multiple families on Christmas and also try to balance life activities with other major feasts. It is essential to acknowledge the devotion of core families, parents who will not only bring children to church for the feast but will take them out of school.

This kind of Orthodox observation of most feasts is similar to the Catholic notion of a day of obligation, where one is technically required to put work and study aside for festal prayer. It is also quite uncommon.

2. For more on opposition to festal vesperal liturgies, see Denysenko, "Liturgical Maximalism," 350–53.

Like most Christians, Orthodox churchgoers attend on some Sundays and on the most solemn feasts (Christmas and Pascha). The majority do not attend the minor feasts and attend a selection of the appointed festal services. Let us take the two most obvious examples, Christmas and Pascha, to reflect on how the ordinary Orthodox Christian participates and how the church might adjust its pastoral strategy.

The ordinary Orthodox Christian is likely to attend one of the services for Christmas and two for Pascha. Depending on family circumstances, parishioners are most likely to attend an evening service on Christmas Eve. Family obligations and domestic preparations require time and energy for most people. The reality for many churchgoers is that they have participated in the Christmas Vigil and not one of the two appointed festal Divine Liturgies.

The circumstances of Pascha are slightly different. Most people will attend one service on Holy Friday and the Matins and Divine Liturgy of Pascha. For many, the Friday evening service is actually the Matins of Holy Saturday, which means that they miss the public proclamation of Christ's passion, crucifixion, death, and burial. Most families will attend the early morning services of Pascha, but the rigorous demands of the services leave some of the youngest and oldest either at home, alone, or in the care of others.

Pastoral Adjustments to Christmas and Pascha

Two adjustments can be applied to both the celebration and the liturgical instruction on Christmas and Pascha that assure churchgoers of their complete partaking of the feasts even if they have attended only one or two services. The primary principle is that the celebration of the Eucharist is the most solemn office, representing the divine life shared by the one who came to make his dwelling among us and who offered himself freely for us and for the life of the world.

The pastoral adjustment for Christmas would be to move the Vesperal Liturgy to the evening hours to enable full participation. Christmas Vespers is rich in Scripture and hymnography, invites popular participation in the psalm refrains, and enables participants to receive Holy Communion. For participants, it would essentially entail participation in one of the two eucharistic services. Large parishes with a strong clergy, singers, and chanters can still have the Vigil later in the evening. This solution is most convenient for smaller to medium-sized parish communities that have the most people attend one service on Christmas Eve.

The dilemma posed on Pascha concerns the timing of the Matins and Divine Liturgy. Most parishes observe these services at midnight, which presents challenges to younger and older people in particular. Orthodox communities in certain regions of the world have Matins and Divine Liturgy at sunrise on Sunday morning, which is no less appropriate than the midnight services.

A simpler solution could have more potential, however. The historical development of the liturgy resulted in two paschal eucharistic liturgies celebrated on Saturday and Sunday. The church customarily celebrates the Paschal Vigil on Saturday, any time between the early morning and the early afternoon. Nocturne, Matins, and Divine Liturgy take place at midnight. The popularity of the midnight services led to a popular distinction between the Paschal Vigil and the midnight offices. An errant explanation emerged that interpreted the Paschal Vigil as one step removed from Pascha, the journey's destination at which the church arrives at midnight. This popular perception is understandable but erroneous; the Paschal Vigil is thoroughly paschal, a veritable greeting and breaking of bread with the risen Lord himself. The full paschal character of the Vigil has positive implications for churchgoers who struggle to attend the midnight offices. The Paschal Vigil gives them a legitimate opportunity to participate fully in the feast. There is neither a prohibition nor a requirement that they also participate in the midnight services.

For both Christmas and Pascha, an adjustment in pastoral instruction will be necessary. The first step is for pastors to accept that there are no inferior or deficient festal Eucharists when two or more are appointed to a feast. The first Eucharist is just as much an encounter with the living God in memory of his birth or resurrection as the second. This step requires pastors to change their thinking on the meaning of the offices appointed to a feast. Each office is a participation in the good news proclaimed on that occasion and is therefore an outpouring of grace in the present. The reception of Holy Communion at one of the eucharistic liturgies breaks bread with God and therefore breaks the fast.

Acceptance of the full quality and character of the first Divine Liturgy of a feast requires pastors to ease their emphasis on the need to participate in all appointed services because they are a progression. While there is certainly some sense of mimetic progression in the seasons leading up to the feasts—the Sundays before Christmas and Holy Week—all of the services give thanks to God for his mighty acts in love of humankind.

Pastors might react to a complication that results from making these adjustments: if one moves the Vesperal Liturgy of St. Basil to the early evening of Christmas Eve, does this compromise the Vigil? Will people be discouraged from attending the Liturgy on Christmas morning? A similar reaction might inhibit pastors from changing their thinking about the Paschal Vigil. If one equates the Vigil with the popular midnight offices, will fewer people participate in the midnight services? Hence, many pastors have a systematic reaction: retain the status quo, and exhort the people to focus their energy on attendance at Pascha, the journey's destiny.

The systemic reaction that privileges keeping things as they have been to preserve tradition is understandable. The rhythm of parish life and community tradition revolves around sustaining beloved rites. Any perceived threat to that rite might be resisted even if the intentions are noble.

Realistically, the chances of losing well-established and beloved traditions are minimal. The risk seems to be a bit lower with the suggested revision to the Christmas cycle of services. The core group of people that observe Christmas at the Vigil and or the morning Divine Liturgy won't change their practices at a whim. People in search of a way to observe the feast liturgically while maintaining their family obligations are the ones most likely to embrace an early evening Vesperal Liturgy on Christmas Eve. A handful of faithful parish adherents might migrate to the early service or perhaps observe both the Vesperal Liturgy and the Vigil.

If people respond positively to the suggested revision, then the church has learned something about herself. The coalescing of a community around a certain service and its appointed time is an affirmation of Jesus' teaching that the Sabbath was made for the people and not the reverse. The liturgy would indeed become pastoral if people embraced the revised order. And if the people rejected or ignored it, then the church learns something about itself yet again—if the people refuse to receive the revision *en masse*, then it is not truly the church's.

The suggestion about Pascha differs because of the ancient and venerable quality and character of the Vigil. The reduction and displacement of the Vigil to the only convenient time on Saturday accommodated the popular midnight services. These services certainly remain popular today, but their appointed time is not compatible with the needs and abilities of the whole church. Reclaiming the paschal character and quality of the Vigil grants a large group of faithful access to the paschal liturgy. Certainly, this revision will require finesse from pastors, who will have to explain that the vigil is indeed Pascha and that proclaiming the resurrection, breaking the eucharistic fast, and partaking in the divine food of the kingdom permits participants to break the dietary fast they have held since the beginning of Lent.

As with Christmas, it is highly unlikely that large hordes of people will abandon the midnight paschal offices for the Paschal Vigil. The already adherent might attend both services, as many already do. The popularity of the midnight offices is not at all at risk of decay—it is much more likely that the church will discover the people who have been hidden from sight and now feel comfortable and able to partake in Pascha fully, without stigma or the perception of deficiency.

The successful implementation of these two pastoral revisions in communities that are most likely to respond favorably reveals two important observations about the principle of progression through a festal period. First, the tendency for pastors to use a sense of progression as a means of exhorting people to attend all of the services lends itself to excluding people who have less access to the local liturgy. While a sense of progression is traditional, it is not essential for pastoral liturgy, as we shall see shortly in our analysis of the liturgical year and time. Pastoral liturgy should be anchored in the Lord's teaching that Sabbath was made for the people. The times for offices and festal celebrations should be appointed in dynamic dialogue with the people's lives. Sometimes, community diversity complicates this planning, but the point remains the same: appoint festal Eucharists to days and times the people are able to observe.

The second observation follows the point on what people can and cannot observe. The historical evolution of the liturgical year produced a great deal of repetition in the services. During Holy Week, many of the same hymns are repeated at other offices, and the same is true of the readings. The two revisions mentioned here would entail two different sets of scriptural lessons for the people. Interestingly, the lessons for the Vesperal Liturgy of Christmas Eve and the Paschal Vigil are more extensive and are delivered through a much broader scriptural scope than those appointed for the more established services. This fact confirms our assertion that participation in one of the festal Eucharists constitutes a full and complete participation in the festal mystery.

THIS IS THE DAY THAT THE LORD HAS MADE

In other words, these services are not deficient. In most cases, then, participation in one part of a festal celebration is both meaningful and transformative even if the traditional scheme of service times has been changed or moved to the nearest Sunday. The same saving God who visited the people in the events commemorated comes again in the present, no matter when that celebration takes place.

The Volume of Hymns: Is Less More?

The next issue is both a problem and an opportunity: the number of hymns appointed to a given feast. The corpus of hymnography appointed to the liturgical year is enormous. The major feasts have several hymns threaded throughout the services, from the troparion and kontakion that express the primary festal themes to stichera chanted with psalm refrains at the Liturgy of the Hours to the festal canons. For most Orthodox theologians and leaders, the festal hymnography is the primary source of the liturgical theology of the feast. I acknowledge the place of privilege held by the hymnography while entreating theologians and pastors to create more space for constructing a liturgical theology of the proclamation of God's word.[3]

There is no question that the festal hymnography is the main repository of patristic reflection on the main feasts of the church. While the kontakion is no longer a poetic sermon performed by a soloist, the current liturgical structures both retain and proclaim the patristic heritage. In addition to the troparion and kontakion, the theotokia chanted on Psalm 140 at Vespers and the festal *doxastika* are rich sources of Orthodox festal liturgical theology.[4]

The process of the history of liturgical development resulted in collecting these hymns and creating methods for selecting them, especially when several themes coincide on a given feast. For a Sunday Divine Liturgy, it is common for a parish to sing four to seven hymns after the entrance (introit). Some parishes will insert hymns in between the verses of the Beatitudes (the third antiphon in the Slavic tradition, just before the entrance).

Some festal celebrations have large collections of hymns. Communities manage them by including only a selection; others sing all of the

---

3. See Andronikof, *Le sens des fêtes*, 7. See also Hannick, "Theotokos in Byzantine," 76.

4. See von Gardner, *Russian Church Singing*, 34–37.

appointed hymns. The services of Holy Week have a particularly large volume, especially the Passion Gospels and Matins of Holy Friday. To put it quite simply, the quantity of hymns is enormous—the services contain more than scriptural lessons.

The performance of the hymns can also be problematic. In some parishes, the choir and chanters sing very quickly in order to sustain a fast pace and avoid prolonging the service. Some smaller parish choirs struggle to sing the music accompanying the hymns, especially since different melodic and harmonic settings are assigned to many in accordance with the Byzantine eight-mode system. Some of the settings are melismatic, making for long, decorated musical performances. Competent intonation and diction are also contributing factors. Managing the workload of a parish's choir and chanters could contribute to more competent vocal performances.

A Three-Part Proposal: Evaluate, Prune, and Plant

Returning briefly to our garden metaphor, I propose that the task presented to the church concerning festal hymns is threefold. First, the church needs to evaluate its corpus of hymns. The evaluation process includes identifying repetitions, removing hymns with anti-Semitic or other questionable tropes, and blessing a system that permits a reasonable selection of hymns to be taken at the feast. Second, the church needs to take steps to remove some hymns that do not express anything new or original or that promote division. Last, the church needs to consider the possibility of composing new hymns for established feasts as well as new ones. We will consider this process of hymn revision through a selection of examples.

Evaluation and Pruning

The Passion Gospels and Matins of Holy Friday provide a helpful example. The service begins with six psalms, the Great Litany, and the Alleluiarion with the appointed troparion. The first Gospel lesson is from John, a lengthy composite requiring about twenty minutes. A series of antiphons consisting of a number of hymns follows the Gospel lesson.

One theme characterizes the hymns belonging to the three antiphons following the first Gospel: Judas is the antagonist, the antihero who betrayed Christ. The same verse concludes each hymn on the third antiphon: "But the wicked Judas pretended not to be aware."[5] The obsession with Judas's treachery does not end with the first Gospel. Following the second, the fourth antiphon takes up the theme yet again and sings "today Judas forsakes the Teacher to embrace the devil."[6] The service continues to emphasize the evil deeds of Judas beyond the second Gospel and its hymns.

This service also includes hymns that might be considered for excision on account of their anti-Semitic tropes. The first hymn of the twelfth antiphon (after the fourth Gospel) is perhaps the most obvious example. The hymn states that Jesus addressed the Jews and accused them of repaying his life-giving acts with crucifixion. The hymn implies that Jesus disavows Israel and instead grants eternal life to the nations.[7]

This brief foray into the Passion Gospels and Matins of Holy Friday touches upon all three of the tasks of the larger objective—evaluate, prune, and plant. The matters of quantity and theme have been addressed and revisions were made to the order and content of this service in the particular version of the office celebrated at the New Skete Monastery.[8] The editors of New Skete's Holy Week acknowledge the "preoccupation with the treachery of Judas" in the liturgical texts of Holy Week.[9] They did not excise the hymns entirely but revised the content so that "other aspects of the season" would not be overwhelmed by the repetitive identification of Judas as the villain of Holy Week.[10] In their evaluation of the Holy Friday service, New Skete describes it as a marathon and a "veritable endurance test" for all participants.[11] The service is long because of its heavy content—dozens of hymns in addition to twelve Gospel lessons.

New Skete's proposed solution to this problem was surgical; they "revamped" the service completely by eliminating many hymns and reducing the number of gospels from twelve to three.[12] The most noticeable revision is to the volume of the service; there is simply less content. The reduction generated more balance in the texts. New Skete did not eliminate references to Judas; the hymns still sing of his treachery. It is also

5. Contos, *Services for Holy Week*, 273–74.

6. Contos, *Services for Holy Week*, 278.

7. Contos, *Services for Holy Week*, 292–93.

8. Monks of New Skete, *Passion and Resurrection*.

9. Monks of New Skete, *Passion and Resurrection*, l.

10. Monks of New Skete, *Passion and Resurrection*, 1.

11. Monks of New Skete, *Passion and Resurrection*, liv.

12. Monks of New Skete, *Passion and Resurrection*, liv–lv.

noteworthy that New Skete retained the hymn expressing anti-Semitic tropes with one significant difference. The New Skete version does not identify the Jews explicitly. It is rearranged so that Jesus addresses "you."[13] An examination of the text leads informed participants to understand that "you" means the Jewish people. Liturgically, however, the people do not hear an explicit reference to Jews. The text includes them in the Lord's reproach ("because of you"), and they are included in the community of God's people as those who crucified him.

The all-inclusive revision of the addressee ("you" instead of "the Jews") accompanies a second smart change; this version of the hymn does not mention transferring the inheritance from the Jews to "the nations." Finally, the placement of this hymn is strategic; it concludes the Matins office before transitioning seamlessly to the tersext. The people hear themselves included in the betrayal as the conclusion to the grand narrative of the Holy Friday service.

One of the problems with the received version of the Holy Friday office is its tendency to assign blame to particular figures and people. New Skete's revisions do not completely eliminate this tendency, but the strategy establishes a stable balance of Scripture and hymn and reduces theological finger pointing. For our purposes, New Skete's revision provides a blueprint of how to execute the task of evaluating and pruning.

The Holy Friday Matins office is an obvious example because of its quantity of material. A similar principle can be applied to other festal liturgies. One way to make the services more manageable is to remove the repetitions built into the hymns. For many feasts, including Christmas and Holy Friday, the hymns appointed to Vespers call for one of the stichera (usually the first) to be repeated one or two times. The objective is to reach the minimal threshold of hymns for the rank of the feast. From the perspective of pastoral liturgy, the repetition of a sticheron is completely unnecessary.

Decisions on omitting hymns appointed by the typikon are more complicated. Some pastors simply make these decisions on the basis of their knowledge of the choir and time constraints. Resistance to limiting the number of hymns comes from pastors and music ministers who value their theological value. This perspective views their omission as constraining the ministry of proclaiming Orthodox theology through music. However, the objective is not to restrain the theological and tropological messages of the hymns. Rather, the matter is quite practical and concerns

---

13. Monks of New Skete, *Passion and Resurrection*, 176–77.

the people's capacity to process and retain the sheer volume of content the hymns express. We have a limited cognitive capacity to retain hymn lyrics.[14] Studies suggest that melodic accompaniment enhances recall, but in general, people tend to remember either the first or the last verse of a given hymn (primacy and recency).[15]

For the purposes of assembling a schedule of festal hymns that inspire, exhort, and teach, a strategic selection of memorable hymns is the best strategy. Expectations must be tempered when creating an order for a service. The musical element is important; people tend to remember shorter verses with the assistance of melody. In this sense, hymns that have a common psalm refrain or short, repeated poetic verses have the most potential for recall.

Church leaders need to temper their expectations on the catechetical impact of a complete hymn. It is highly unlikely that people will recall the middle sections of texts, which tend to carry the most theological material. To be sure, the most devout—those completely attuned to the liturgical order—are more likely to engage more liturgical material from sermons to hymns.[16] Those who are less familiar with the liturgical tradition have a lower capacity for engaging and retaining material.[17] In other words, the maximal liturgical approach is for the most ardent insiders, those who attend all celebrations and have a high level of interest in them. Recall and retention are limited even within this group. If the pastoral strategy is to engage as much of the participating congregation as possible, then it is essential to prioritize shorter and more memorable hymns—the kinds that people tend to hum in the car on the way home from church.

Ideology and Conceptions of God, Mary, and the Saints

Select portions of this study have yielded insights into the formation and meaning of feasts like the Elevation of the Cross on September 14, St. Gregory Palamas, and the Baptism of Rus.' Liturgical components from these services recall specific events that incorporate the prevalence of empires into the liturgy. The hymns of the feast of the Exaltation repeatedly refer to

14. On this matter, see Overstreet and Healy, "Item and Order."

15. Maylor, "Serial Position," 819.

16. On this matter, see the older study by Pargament and DeRosa, "Predicting Memory," 189–90.

17. See Maylor, "Serial Position," 817.

Christ as the king and recall the appearance of the true cross (at the Battle of the Milvian Bridge) to the Emperor Constantine.[18]

The service to St. Gregory on the second Sunday of Lent contains several texts that praise him for defending Orthodoxy and defeating the heretics and Barlaam through his teaching.[19] The Baptism of Rus' exalts St. Volodymyr for his apostolic witness and identifies Rus' with contemporary Russia in some translations. Icon feasts present a unique dilemma; on the one hand, they honor the people's testimony that God is with us, in our very midst, in the present. On the other, they have occasionally provided fodder for church leaders to use them as evangelical tools.

The application of historical events of the past by the present community is the first issue. Feasts anchored in the scriptural narrative are of less concern here, especially if the lectionary functions as the primary source of festal liturgical theology. The issue becomes more complicated with some aspects of Marian feasts. Mary's identity as the strong defender of the imperial capital, a theme that migrated from Constantinople to a number of locations in Rus', exposes a thin line separating Mary as an intercessor before God's throne and Mary as the defender of God's chosen Orthodox people.[20]

The troparion appointed to the Exaltation and the third Sunday of Lent beseeches God to save his people and grant them victory over their adversaries. The church calls upon Mary to protect her people. Events taking place after the New Testament era are the primary contributors of themes like these to the festal narrative. These matters require pastoral attention when they inspire questions within and outside of the church. What does the church mean when it sings "exalt the horn of Thy Orthodox people" or "most holy Theotokos, save us"?

Experts in historical and liturgical theology have the heuristic tools to make sense of such texts and petitions. The authors of hagiographical and hymnographical narratives wrote from the perspective of their contexts. From the Christian imperial perspective, the emperor was anointed by God, and the citizens of the empire were therefore under God's protection. There was no need to manipulate the texts to offer a spiritual explanation of their meaning. On this matter, we agree with Sean Griffin's assessment; the cross

18. "The Cross of the Giver of Life appeared in the heavens to the godly King"(*Festal Menaion*, 137).

19. See, for example, a sessional hymn after "Ode 3" of the canon at Matins in *Lenten Triodion*, 320.

20. See the text of the doxastikon at the Dormition in *Festal Menaion*, 507.

is a weapon designed to drive away political enemies.[21] The church recorded eyewitness accounts of Mary defending her people from their adversaries with force in various places. The authors of these texts did not hesitate to enter these accounts into the historical and liturgical narratives.

The ethical issue that emerges here concerns the transmission of Christian political ideologies into the present. The liturgical texts take Orthodox imperialism for granted. Orthodox Christians are God's chosen people, and the texts suggest that the cross and Mary's intercession can and will literally defend them from their enemies. Some texts continue to advocate for the restoration of monarchical political structures because they are ordained by God.[22] A selection of these texts depicts the Orthodox as an exceptional community. When neighboring states act aggressively towards a state with an Orthodox majority, they are justified in responding with force because the texts suggest that God blesses the use of force in response. The tendency to adopt an identity of religious superiority is another problem. Texts like these can lend themselves to harmful othering, viewing the non-Orthodox as adversarial and interpreting criticism as aggression.[23] Liturgical texts can become part of a larger metanarrative imposing a reactive, defiant, and defensive identity on the Orthodox. This attitude can become sectarian and dangerous if pastors do not take corrective action.[24]

One objection to this problem is that aggressive exceptionalism is rare. Many pastors attend to this issue by presenting spiritual or historical explanations of such texts. The cross is a weapon to be yielded against demons, not other people. Demons are the adversaries to be defeated. Petitions to the Theotokos to save us are actually referring to deliverance from sin. Examples of historical interpretations include sermons and speeches that celebrate the feast of the Baptism of Rus' as a joyous occasion for the contemporary heirs of Kyivan Rus', not as an appeal to reconstitute medieval Rus' in some form.

Wise pastors have the tools for interpreting such texts for a modern Orthodox audience. Our response to the objection in the preceding

21. Griffin, *Liturgical Past*, 161–62.

22. See the third troparion on "Ode 8" of the canon to St. John of Shanghai and San Francisco, *Service and Akathist*, 26.

23. Two seminal collections of essays discuss this issue. See Demacopoulos and Papanikolaou, eds., *Orthodox Constructions*; and Krawchuk and Bremer, *Eastern Orthodox Encounters*.

24. For a case study on the potential dangers of harmful othering through exploitation of the official liturgy, see Denysenko, "Dignity and Conflict."

paragraph is that the people should not require a mechanism assisting them in interpreting a text inherited from the past. Petitions and hymns are living, sung and offered in the present and not reducible to an encomium to the past. If texts should be accessible and comprehensible, as argued here, then the church can select from a number of options to protect the liturgy from becoming a source for dubious ideologies. The first option is surgery: simply remove the texts that could contribute to the formation of a dubious ideology. Surgically removing some of these texts could violate the integrity of the feast by attempting to erase the past. Revising some of the liturgical texts could be a more effective strategy. For example, the petitions that conclude many of the hymns might be altered so that they proclaim "deliver us from the evil one" instead of "deliver us from our enemies." Some of the petitions to Mary might ask her to "pray to God for us" instead of "save us." Intensive revision or new compositions could better represent the meaning of a feast for the contemporary Orthodox Church. It is both possible and legitimate to narrate and praise Constantine and Volodymyr for their acts without petitioning for the restoration of an emperor or victory over political adversaries and enemies. It is likewise laudable to proclaim St. Gregory Palamas's teachings on the essence and energies of God without repeatedly exulting in Barlaam's and the heretics' defeat. The third option is the one most pastors would be likely to adopt. Theologians can create a catechetical program for pastors that assists them in explaining how the present church understands its past.[25] Such a program could be beneficial in communicating that in the twenty-first century, Orthodox Christians are not required to recreate the past. Petitions asking God from deliverance from enemies do not mean that they cannot befriend people of other churches and religions. Selecting the third option fails to remove the unnecessary extra step of explaining texts that might be obtuse for some. A better approach is to revise existing texts or compose new ones that honor the past without requiring the church to rebuild its structures or sustain its ideologies.

Icon Feasts and the Problem of Commodification

Christians have struggled with the tendency to commodify liturgy and sacraments for centuries. Papal indulgences and stipends for private masses are the most notorious historical examples. A lesser known but

---

25. This hypothetical program would be ideally created and presented by a group of liturgical theologians in cooperation with church representatives.

equally problematic problem is the practice of commodifying icon feasts. The temptation with icon feasts and relics is not limited to generating false hope for miraculous healings and good fortune. Using them as the dangling of a promise for healing promotes liturgical causality. If you pray for it, God will grant it.

One might object to this statement of a problem by arguing that Jesus instructs his disciples to make their petitions with the expectation that God will grant them. Like the stories of Mary's intercessions in history, readers will state that God, Mary, and the saints appear to their people through icons and relics. The following argument does not deny instances of such epiphanies and theophanies, especially since I have both witnessed and received anointing from multiple relics and icons. The issue at hand is the messaging. The occasion for each icon feast is the same: an epiphany or the appearance of Jesus, Mary, or a saint. Epiphanies are the sources of sacred topography; a place becomes holy because God (or one of God's saints) has appeared in the midst of the people. In this sense, icons and relics constitute a second layer of sacred topography. The difference is that the epiphany takes place through the icon or relic. Occasions like these are revelatory, signs of God's love for his people. They are holy and worthy of festal gathering whether or not miracles were performed on the occasion of the appearance. As we have seen, in many places these miracles have taken place—exorcisms, healings, the restoration of fertility, conversion, and repentance. God has always blessed people through material agency—fire, water, oil, soil, bread, wine. The myrrh that streams from icons and relics tangibly manifests God's presence and love. None of these characteristics cause problems.

Problems surface when the occasion for gathering shifts from thanksgiving for God's gracious appearance to the possibility of a miracle through an event. Stories circulate of people suffering from various calamities who came to venerate the icon or relic and received healing. When the icon feast is celebrated, and when the icon goes on tour to foreign cities, people flock to the liturgical gathering with the hope that God will perform a miracle. Many depart from those gatherings thinking that their prayers have gone unanswered. Sick relatives die, relations remain strained, illnesses persist, men and women remain unable to conceive children. Lost in this forest of miraculous icons are the attributes of God. God remains the lover of humankind, just in healing and in sickness, in life and in death, in flourishing and in poverty. The prayers were answered, but in some cases, those who sent up the prayer received something other than what they had requested.

Icon feasts become commodified when the purpose of the gathering is to use the possibility of a miracle to draw people to the church. The only purpose for the assembly is to remember and give thanks for the theophanies and epiphanies that took place at the original event and to ask God and the saints to once again dwell among God's people. Customs like distributing copies of icons, anointing with myrrh, and praying for people who offer payment for a vigil lamp before the wonder-working icon or relic straddle the line between authentic liturgical piety and commodification. Praying with icons and receiving anointing are venerable Christian traditions. Using any of these traditions to offer promises that cannot be guaranteed or to add revenue crosses the line from piety into commodification. Timothy Brunk has demonstrated persuasively that contemporary consumer culture has distorted the Christian approach to the sacraments. He explains the simple and helpful distinction between gift and commodity.[26] The commodity can become a tool used at our discretion, a choice to use or discard. A gift is given to the recipient with the trust and confidence that they will use it responsibly.

One might add that gifts are not merely taken; they are received with gratitude, and the thankfulness extends beyond simply putting the gift aside or exchanging it for something better. The gift offered to Christians in icon feasts is an appearance of God or the saints that communicates the promise to be with and among us. This is the only promise—to be with the people—and the only proper response is thanksgiving, followed by a petition to be among us.

Liturgical Time: Past, Present, Future, and a Particular People

The final matter at hand is the question of time. Two aspects of liturgical studies in particular raise questions about the relationship between the liturgy and time: the Liturgy of the Hours, and the liturgical year. The bulk of liturgical study on the liturgical year explores the history of feasts. Scholars connect feasts and seasons to anthropology: the way people lived, especially the rhythms of agrarian cultures and the solar cycles.[27]

26. Brunk, *Sacraments and Consumer*, 76–79.

27. See contributions by Wainwright, "Sacramental Time"; Streza, "Orthodox

The theological perspective on the liturgical year places less emphasis on chronology and more on the mystery underpinning every feast. A kind of theological consensus has emerged on the meaning of any given feast. Each feast is the church's participation in the great mystery of Christ and the promise of his second coming. Matias Augé beautifully describes the relationship between a feast observed in time with the telos of Christian life. The liturgical year is a time that "repeats itself like a spiral progressing toward the Parousia."[28] Augé explains the liturgical year through the metaphor of ascending a mountain; at the summit, one meets Christ himself.[29] Robert Taft affirms Augé's assertion and writes that the purpose of the liturgical year—and of anamnesis in general—is to lead Christians to Christ as he is now.[30] Taft explains that the apostolic church did not desire a return to the time of Jesus before his Passover but yearned for the fulfillment of time, to be with Christ as they encountered him after the resurrection. Taft represents a cohort of theologians who view the liturgical year as the coming together of the past, present, and future. Observing the feast is not only a foretaste of eternity but the experience of Christ's life in us.[31]

This theology of the liturgical year instructs Christians to honor the past but not to recreate or dwell upon it. The feasts of the liturgical year are not supposed to be a communal rhapsodizing about the way things were once upon a time in the past. The liturgical year captures and expresses the synergy of anamnesis and epiclesis that takes place in every liturgical gathering, especially the Sunday eucharistic assembly.

Is there a gap between the theology of the liturgical year so eloquently explained by the likes of Augé and Taft and the experience of the community that gathers for the occasion? The liturgical theology of any given feast delivers the same promise—God is with us, and all will be well. If this is the case, and if each feast is a micro-level instance of what the community prays on Sunday, what is special about the liturgical year?

The feasts of the liturgical year bring the power of communal memory into focus. There are three features that are unique to the liturgical year and confirm its prominent place in Christian tradition. First, it broadens and elaborates the narrative of salvation history that is simply impossible

---

Liturgical Year."

28. Augé, "Theology of the Liturgical Year," 322.

29. Augé, "Theology of the Liturgical Year," 322.

30. Taft, *Beyond East and West*, 24.

31. Taft, *Beyond East and West*, 27.

within the structure of a Sunday eucharistic assembly. The complete narrative provides an opportunity for the local and universal church to receive the full blessings of anamnesis. Community narratives are essential for tradition, and they have the capacity to form generations of faithful. Devoting the time to hearing the story of Christ, Mary, or a beloved saint strengthens the bonds of communion between Christians of the present and those on the other side of the kingdom. It is not just the stories themselves, powerful as they may be; the rituals involved in sharing the narrative with the next generation enable the hearers to be adopted into the ongoing story. The Serbian *Krsna Slava* captures this idea by inviting the next generation of family members to come under the patronage of the saint who adopted their family of origin.

Particularity is the second feature that characterizes the uniqueness of the liturgical year. Many feasts are strongly associated with particular communities. In many cases, a saint or event that originated with a native community came to be adopted universally. It is essential, however, to maintain a sense of the native particularity when understanding why feasts appointed to particular dates are so important. Many of the dates correspond with the native community's memory of original events. While some have strong theological resonances (like Christmas), any attempt to change them now would be met with fierce resistance, because communities have become accustomed to centering their lives around them.

Questions about the inner logic of a date are diminished in importance when one considers the power of community memory. Numerous feasts are products of that particularity, the intimacy shared between a community of origin and the holy figure they remember. Thomas Talley explains the significance of community memory when he describes festivals as times of "heightened religious consciousness."[32] The power of presence retained by a community invokes other memories, a factor that contributes to the expansion of a feast into a mini liturgical season. Particularity accompanies the elaboration of the memorial narrative in this scheme.

The final issue concerns challenges with the liturgical year. The first challenge is the potential gap between the blessings people receive at feasts—communion with God and the saints now, in the present—and the tendency to convert feasts into a rhapsodizing of the past. Pastors confront many challenges with feasts rooted in rich anamnesis. The first is the tendency to idealize the past without sufficient attention to how God is

32. Talley, *Origins of the Liturgical Year*, 237.

working in the present. Pastors must craft their preaching and construct liturgical environments in such a way so that participants know that this story is as much about them as it is about the historical figures of the narrative. Liturgical scholars emphasize the frequent use of the word "today" in festal celebration as opposed to "at that time."[33] Today's liturgical participants are called to become God's servants on the basis of their witness to the narrative handed down to them. The second issue is the matter of time as a commodity. Lizette Larson-Miller suggests that consumerism has distorted special occasions and holy seasons and feasts by converting them into invitations to consume.[34] The result of this overwhelming cultural phenomenon is a crisis of insatiability; consuming does not fulfill, no matter how vigorously one pursues it.

We have seen that numerous factors have contributed to the formation of the liturgical year. One may ask questions about liturgical overgrowth and the demands of this or that season or feast. The liturgical year would continue to demand anticipation and vigilance even if a surgical approach to pruning some of its seasons were applied. Larson-Miller reminds us that inculturation is a two-way street; engaging in the waiting and patience required by the seasons and feasts is an essential act of preparing for eternal life with the triune God.[35]

The feasts of the year deliver on that promise with a special intensity. Any given feast of the liturgical year is a paradox. A community gathers to remember a holy person and event in time, and the eternal one enters into that time and dwells with the community. Orthodox Christians join all others in viewing these instances of communion with God as tastes of the destiny of humankind, the restoration of all to God in Christ. It is this experience of communion *in time* that transforms the desire of consumerism into a desire for life shared with God in paradise. It is not a matter of a feast making time holy; for Christians, the liturgical year is all about the humility of God, who enters into time so that he can be with us. Each feast affords the opportunity to be with God in that particular kind of intensity, rooted in the memory of forbears.

33. This is especially true in the context of liturgical anamnesis that establishes epiclesis. On this dynamic, see Irwin, *Context and Text*, 73–77.

34. Larson-Miller, "Consuming Time," 538.

35. Larson-Miller, "Consuming Time," 539.

Conclusion

T HIS ANALYSIS OF THE liturgical year in the Orthodox Church has emphasized meaning. Our review brings us full circle to the leading question: What is the liturgical year? A recap of the study's main observations establishes a starting point for the final analysis.

Sacred Topography

The liturgical year originated through assemblies that commemorated sacred events in particular places. Sacred topography is therefore one of its primary features. Gathering in the specific place associated with the original event enhances the particularity of the occasion. Holy Week and Pascha were intense in Jerusalem because it was the location of Jesus' passion, death, and resurrection. The construction of a church complex in and around the events enhanced the particularity, as Egeria's fourth-century report reminds us.

This sense of sacred topography is a blueprint for many feasts, including the Transfiguration of Christ, the Dormition of Mary in Gethsemane, and especially the *dies natalis* that provided occasion for the commemoration of a local saint. The local quality of the original saving events of Christ, Mary, and the saints was connected directly to the sense of particularity. Christ was crucified "here," and pastors used sacred topography for exhortation, to remind people that they are standing on holy ground.

The Impact of Theology on the Development
of the Liturgical Year

Numerous factors have influenced the expansion of the liturgical year. Christmas emerged as a distinct feast for theological reasons, as evidenced by Justinian's imposition of the feast on the Church of Jerusalem in the sixth century. Theology inspired the Sunday commemorations of the ecumenical councils, including the first on the Sunday after Ascension. The Sundays honoring Saints Gregory Palamas, St. John Climacus, and St. Mary of Egypt represent the monastic stewardship of the liturgy and their affinity for right theology (St. Gregory) and the ascetical life (St. John and Mary).

Theology also inspired important Marian commemorations like the "Akathistos Hymn," now sung on the fifth Saturday of Lent and often on preceding weeks. The poetic verses of the "Akathistos Hymn" go far beyond honoring Mary for her faithful assent to God's will, her giving birth to Christ, and the testimony of her holy life before and after birth. The hymn glorifies Mary as an intercessor with the power to intervene and defend Christians from all afflictions, including sickness, invasion, civil war, and natural disasters. The mythology of Mary's intervention went on its own trajectory and became part of the "Akathistos Hymn" as well as other festal narratives, such as those of the Dormition and Protection.

Ideology in the Liturgical Year

Often, feasts evolved into commemorations that differ from their original blueprint. The Exaltation of the Cross became a feast feting the empire, the reign of kings, and victory over adversaries. The Baptism of Rus' shifted from the celebration of a baptism of citizens of a city-state to another example of holy rulers (Volodymyr following Constantine's example) and the utopia of a particular holy nation. Ideology assumed control from theology in determining the meaning of a feast.

Festal Intensity and the Expansion of Mini-Cycles

Feasts are intense experiences of encounter. Two aspects of this intensity have contributed to the experience of the liturgical year. The power of memory and experience elongated certain festal celebrations. Certain feasts became festal periods, ranging from a second day and including octaves and forty days. The church drew from the biblical precedent of periods to assign festal seasons. The appointment of forty days to Lent, the Christmas Fast, the cycle of incarnational feasts, and the period from Pascha to Ascension constitutes an ecclesial appropriation of biblical precedents. Eschatology contributes to festal periods in the assignment of octaves and the fifty days of Pentecost.

The key here is the intensity of solemnity. The intensity with which solemn feasts are experienced by the community tends to be extended over a period of time. The church has responded to this intensity by adding new commemorations to certain feasts. The gradual growth of the pre-Lenten Sundays and the synaxes of Mary (December 26), John the Baptist (January 7), and Symeon and Anna (February 3) exemplify this growth.

Universal Adoption of Local Commemorations

The evolution of feasts from local to universal commemorations is the final feature of the liturgical year. Pilgrimages and the transfer and gifting of relics have facilitated the sharing of a saint. Visitors and dignitaries brought relics home and installed them in appointed objects or places in their churches as the new community adopted the saint as their own. Orthodox churches throughout the world continue this trend, which explains why a local saint like Maria Skobtsova of Paris can be honored by communities in any and every place.

The phenomena that ignited the expansion of the liturgical year also created some problems. We have addressed many of these issues in this study. Perhaps the most glaring problem is pastoral: What constitutes complete observation of a feast? The intensity of solemnity has expanded the periods surrounding certain feasts. The Paschal Triduum has five long and intense liturgical offices that contain multiple repetitions of Scripture and song all before the first celebration of the paschal Eucharist.

Pastoral Problem: How Much Observation is Enough?

The intensity of the experience has driven pastors to interpret festal periods as progressive. In other words, it is not enough to attend one service on Holy Friday. Pastors demand that Orthodox Christians attend all of the services of the festal cycle, as missing any one of them results in an incomplete experience. External factors figure into the pastoral expectation—a parish's seasonal budget depends on robust giving, especially for the cycle of Christmas and paschal services.

In this study, I have argued that church communities that serve large populations have been responsible for the clusters of services. Monastic communities with rhythms built around a regular liturgical cycle have had both the clergy and singers for a more extensive festal cycle. The situation for a medium-sized parish is different. For most parishes, the same people sing, with one priest and possibly a deacon available to assist.

One Eucharist Is Complete Participation

We have suggested that the blueprint provided by the cathedral and monastic heritage of the church can be revised. If a parish has more than one Eucharist marking a major feast, participation in one of these services should be considered complete and breaks the preparatory fast. Pascha, Christmas, and Theophany are the most apt examples.

The challenge here to pastors is twofold. First, they must perform the mental gymnastics required to view one Eucharist—or even one liturgical office—as a complete observance of the feast. Second, pastors will have to muster up the courage required to inform the people that participating in the Vesperal Liturgy of Christmas or the Paschal Vigil are equivalent to participating in the Liturgy on Christmas morning or Pascha at midnight. Perhaps the opportunity to fold people who have been excluded from participation into the festal celebration by scheduling services at times that match their schedules will motivate clergy to adopt this new mindset.

This study also addressed three additional problems resulting from the historical evolution of the liturgical year: the ideological exploitation of certain feasts, the commodification of icon feasts, and the disconnect between the volume of hymnography and the people's capacity to process and retain the theology expressed by hymns. Like the problem of viewing a festal season as a progression, resolving these problems necessitates the adoption of a new mindset.

Principle of Festal Interpretation: Thanksgiving for Epiphanies

Ideology can be mitigated by removing nostalgia and adopting an eschatological view of a given feast. In some cases, the removal of hymns that are easily misconstrued as nostalgic and the composition of new liturgical content could contribute to a solution. The commodification of icon feasts and visitations occurs when church leaders sensationalize miraculous healings, knowing that people will be drawn to the possibility of a miracle. Icon feasts are new epiphanies, manifestations of God and divine love for God's people in the present. Reorienting these commemorations as thanksgiving for God's presence and petitions for God to continue to be with his people can be the new mindset on these feasts.

The Privileged Place of Hymnography and Liturgical Balance

The problem of the volume of hymnography cannot be easily resolved. Most scholars rightfully identify hymnography as the primary living repository of patristic preaching. Because of hymnography's venerable reputation, the church tends to adopt the principle of embracing the existing liturgy as opposed to transforming the liturgy to meet the people.[1]

This study adopts a minority view and calls for a thorough review of the extant hymnography with a significant reduction in the number of hymns appointed to the services. Our reasoning is twofold. First, we contend that the lectionary is and remains the primary source of liturgical theology for each feast. In the received tradition, the appointed hymnography monopolizes festal interpretation. A reduction in it would create more balance between Scripture and poetry. Second, psychological studies expose the limitations of hymnography's catechetical capacity. People simply do not retain large volumes of words, and those who retain more tend to occupy the inner circle of the church. This appeal does not aim to remove hymnography but to prune it so that the other liturgical components—Scripture, euchology, rite, gesture, and art—are not muted by the sheer amount of poetry.

What Is the Liturgical Year?

The liturgical year is a macrocosm of the celebration of each Divine Liturgy. The ordinary Divine Liturgy is an act of anamnesis and epiclesis, remembering God's mighty acts, the intercessions of Mary and the saints, and calling upon God to deepen our communion with him in the kingdom

1. See Pott, *Byzantine Liturgical Reform*, 43–46.

that has arrived. The similarity of the ordinary Divine Liturgy with the liturgical year begs our final question: Is the liturgical year necessary? Our response is an enthusiastic yes, and we conclude this book by explaining why the liturgical year is not only necessary but how we might truly renew its celebration in the twenty-first century.

Raising the possibility of renewing the liturgical year generates any number of reactions. For centuries, the church's first selection from the list of possibilities has been to attempt to convert people to the existing practices. In the early twentieth century, Russian bishops encouraged deaneries and parishes to bring the opulent ritual celebrations into the public square. The ecumenical liturgical movement of the twentieth century focused on the *ars celebrandi* as the key to liturgical renewal. The notion that the liturgical movement was minimalist and reductionistic is mistaken. The movement encouraged new symbols, music, and sacred art that represented the global nature of the church. The objective was not to replace older functions with new ones but to execute the existing ministries with competence and love. Opposing liturgical schools of thought could agree on certain principles. For example, the Russian Orthodox Church Outside of Russia (ROCOR) rejected the possibility of excising liturgical structures and components, whereas New Skete Monastery embraced and implemented a surgical approach. Despite their differences, they shared the core liturgical values of presiding with dignity and singing the appointed hymns competently and for the comprehension of the people.

We have presented our rationale for making necessary revisions to the liturgical year. These revisions are not enough, on their own, to renew the liturgical year in the life of the church. Issuing grave announcements about the moral consequences of not observing the liturgical year is a strategy that has failed for decades. Pastors have also attempted to affix adult education to the liturgy. This, too, is a noble idea but misunderstands the purpose of the liturgy and should be avoided.[2]

The Liturgical Year: About People, Not Time

The liturgical year can be renewed if the church rediscovers its ecclesiological nature. Most theological analysis and reflection on the church year obsesses about time in order to explain the rationale for the appointment of dates and the inner logic of mini festal cycles. These explanations

2. See Kavanagh, *Elements of Rite*, 101–2.

contribute to the thinking that the liturgical year is about time. Earlier, this analysis affirmed the ecumenical synthesis of the liturgical year; it is a commemoration that brings the future and past together in the present. The liturgical year is an exercise of the classic symbiosis of anamnesis and epiclesis. The assembly thanks God for God's mighty acts and asks God to pour out divine grace again, now as then. Liturgical anamnesis is not an expression of gratitude for a period of time. Anamnesis is thanksgiving offered to a person who is alive and among us in the present.

The liturgical year, then, is not really about time; it is about the people who constitute communities of love. The assemblies gather on an appointed date to celebrate a living person. The most suitable analogy for a feast day is the celebration of one's birthday. The annual celebration happens on the same date and involves diverse rituals, preparation, and eager anticipation. A birthday shares two central features with feasts of the liturgical year. First, it is in honor of a living person. Second, the birthday is a threshold rite; it marks a deepening of passage through one's life and, on certain occasions, like the sixteenth and fiftieth birthdays, the beginning of a new stage of life.

Feasts are Extraordinary Events

Feasts of the liturgical year are similar to Sundays. The difference is the additional level of festive intensity. For Orthodox Christians, feast days are strong moments of encounter with the living God and the communion of saints in heaven and on Earth. Certainly, some observe the liturgical year out of a sense of duty. For many, the memory of a strong past encounter inspires them to return to the next. In such moments, the material and the spiritual come together just as heaven and earth do. Songs, art, smells, and rites are mindful of past encounters and bring participants together for the next.

It is in this sense—the capacity for a strong encounter—that the liturgical year is truly extraordinary. The core stories proclaimed by the Scriptures are the primary sources of meaning not because of some academic rule but because of the power of sharing a story. The scriptural lessons always have the capacity to change the lives of participants because their proclamation conveys God's divine love. Many have heard these stories and accepted the invitation to become part of the unfolding of God's story. The liturgical year can be renewed in the twenty-first century and beyond if we come to appreciate it as an opportunity to be folded into the story of God. This is why each feast day has the capacity to become a threshold rite; if we embrace the opportunity to come, hear the story, and join the community in offering thanksgiving and petition, we can take another step in the journey of Christian life that leads us to Christ himself, along with Mary and the communion of saints.

Finally, another everyday analogy confirms the inner meaning of the Orthodox liturgical year. To put it quite simply, it is a special occasion. The feast day is not like every other day. Observing the feast day is not a matter of duty or obligation. It is not to gain exclusive access to the sacred time reserved for holy people. It is quite the opposite, because the feast day is an all-inclusive occasion, the opportunity for all to come, see, and meet Christ, Mary, and the saints.

Where Is the Holy City? Wherever the Church Gathers

The ancient symbiosis of local and universal on the liturgical calendar rounds out this final reflection. Throughout Christian history, the original locations of theophanies and the native sites of saints have been renowned as holy places. The dedication of churches in these places has created a sacred topography and local veneration has become a magnet for pilgrims in search of the holy. This phenomenon remains vibrant in contemporary Orthodoxy. People make pilgrimages to the Holy Land and travel to famous monasteries in search of spiritual direction and forgiveness. The liturgical year makes sacred topography universal by the power of the Holy Spirit. Each place becomes Jerusalem when it gathers in memory of Christ and his saint, no matter how nondescript. It is this continual act of God reaching out to God's people, wherever and whoever they are, that expresses this inner meaning of the Orthodox liturgical year and, indeed, of all Christian feasts.

Bibliography

Adam, Adolf. *The Liturgical Year: Its History and Its Meaning after the Reform of the Liturgy.* Translated by Matthew J. O'Connell. Collegeville, MN: Liturgical, 1981.

Alexopoulos, Stefanos. *The Presanctified Liturgy in the Byzantine Rite: A Comparative Analysis of Its Origins, Evolution, and Structural Components.* Leuven, Belgium: Peeters, 2009.

Andronikof, Constantin. *Le sens des fêtes.* Paris: Éditions du Cerf, 1970.

Antofijchuk, Volodymyr. "Різдво Христове в Українській обрядовій і вербальній культурі." *Буковинський журнал* (2007) 175–80.

Antoninus, Johann Gildemeister. *Antonini Placentini Itinerarium.* Berlin: H. Reuther, 1889.

Arranz, Miguel. "Les 'fêtes théologiques du calendrier byzantine.'" In *La liturgie, expression de la foi,* edited by Achille M. Triacca and Alessandro Pistoia, 29–55. Rome: Edizioni Liturgiche, 1979.

———. "Les prières de la gonyklisia ou de la génuflexion du jour de la Pentecôte dans l'ancien Euchologe byzantine." *Orientalia christiana periodica* 48, no. 1 (1982) 92–123.

———. "Les sacrements de l'ancien euchologe constantinopolitain." *Orientalia christiana periodica* 49, no. 1 (1983) 42–90.

Aubineau, Michel. *Les homélies festales d'Hésychius de Jérusalem.* Brussels, Belgium: Société des Bollandistes, 1978.

Augé, Matias. "A Theology of the Liturgical Year." In *Handbook for Liturgical Studies,* vol. 5, *Liturgical Time and Space,* edited by Anscar J. Chupungco, 317–30. Collegeville, MN: Liturgical, 2000.

Balashov, Nicolai. *На пути к литургическому возрождению.* Moscow: Round Table on Religious Education and Service, 2001.

Bertonière, Gabriel. *The Historical Development of the Easter Vigil and Related Services in the Greek Church.* Orientalia Christiana Analecta, 193. Rome: Institutum Studiorum Orientalium, 1972.

———. *Sundays of Lent in the Triodion: The Sundays without a Commemoration.* Rome: Pontificio Istituto Orientale, 1997.

Bobrinskoy, Boris. "Ascension and Liturgy: The Ascension and High Priesthood of Christ in Relation to Worship." *St. Vladimir's Seminary Quarterly* 3, no. 4 (Fall 1959) 11–28.

Bradshaw, Paul F., and Maxwell E. Johnson. *The Origins of Feasts, Fasts and Seasons in Early Christianity.* Collegeville, MN: Liturgical, 2011.

Brock, Sebastian P. "Some Important Baptismal Themes in the Syriac Tradition." In *The Harp,* edited by V. C. Samuel, Geevarghese Panicker, and Rev. Jacob Thekeparampil. Piscataway, NJ: Gorgias, 2012.

Brown, Peter. *The Cult of the Saints: Its Rise and Function in Latin Christianity.* The Haskell Lectures on History of Religions New Series, No. 2. Chicago: University of Chicago Press, 1981.

Brunk, Timothy. *The Sacraments and Consumer Culture.* Collegeville, MN: Liturgical, 2020.

Buchinger, Harald. "On the Origin and Development of the Liturgical Year: Tendencies, Results, and Desiderata of Heortological Research." *Studia Liturgica* 40 (2010) 14–45. https://doi.org/10.1177/0039320710040001-202.

Calivas, Alkiviadis C. *Great Week and Pascha in the Greek Orthodox Church.* Brookline, MA: Holy Cross Orthodox, 1992.

———. *The Liturgy in Dialogue: Exploring and Renewing the Tradition.* Vol. 5, *Essays in Theology and Liturgy.* Brookline, MA: Holy Cross Orthodox, 2018.

Chrysostom, John. *De Baptismo Christi.* In *Patrologia Graeca 49,* edited by J.-P. Migne, 365–66. Paris: Migne, 1862.

Служба святому равноапостольному князю Владимиру. Свято-Владимирский Храм (Website). November 1, 2021. http://svhram.info/index.php/o-khrame/ nebesnyj-pokrovitel/item/16-служба-святому-князюю-владимиру.

Climacus, John. *The Ladder of Divine Ascent.* Omaha, NE: Patristic, 2020.

Contos, Leonidas C. *Services for Holy Week and Easter (Orthodox).* Northridge, CA: Narthex, 1993.

de Strycker, Émile. "Le Protévangile de Jacques: Problèmes critiques et exégétiques." In *Studia Evangelica 3,* edited by F. L. Cross, 339–59. Berlin: Akademie Verlag, 1964.

Demacopoulos, George, and Aristotle Papanikolaou, eds. *Orthodox Constructions of the West.* New York: Fordham University Press, 2013.

Denysenko, Nicholas. "An Appeal to Mary: An Analysis of Pussy Riot's Punk Performance in Moscow." *Journal of American Academy of Religion* 81, no. 4 (December 2013) 1061–92.

———. "Baptismal Themes in the Byzantine Blessing of Waters on Theophany." *Logos: A Journal of Eastern Christian Studies* 52 (2011) 55–88.

———. *The Blessing of Waters and Epiphany: The Eastern Liturgical Tradition.* Burlington, VT: Ashgate, 2012.

———. "Chaos in Ukraine: The Churches and the Search for Leadership." *International Journal for the Study of the Christian Church* 14, no. 3 (September 2014) 242–59.

———. "Dignity and Conflict: Religious Violence. In *Value and Vulnerability: An Interfaith Dialogue on Human Dignity,* edited by Jonathan Rothchild, and Matthew R. Petrusek, 324–51. Notre Dame, IN: University of Notre Dame Press, 2020.

———. "Liturgical Maximalism in Orthodoxy: A Case Study." *Worship* 87 (2013) 338–62.

———. *The People's Faith: The Liturgy of the Faithful in Orthodoxy.* Lanham, MD: Lexington, 2018.

———. "Psalm 81: Announcing the Resurrection on Holy Saturday." *Logos: A Journal of Eastern Christian Studies* 50, nos. 1–2 (2009) 55–88.

———. "Rituals and Prayers of Forgiveness in Byzantine Lent." *Worship* 86 (2012) 150–59.

Destivelle, Hyacinthe. *The Moscow Council (1917–1918): The Creation of the Conciliar Institutions of the Russian Orthodox Church.* Notre Dame, IN: University of Notre Dame Press, 2015.

Devonshire Jones, Tom, et al. "Martyrium." *The Oxford Dictionary of Christian Art and Architecture.* Oxford University Press. Retrieved July 26, 2022. https://www.oxfordreference.com/view/10.1093/acref/9780199680276.001.0001/acref-9780199680276-e-1133.

Doig, Allan. *Liturgy and Architecture: From the Early Church to the Middle Ages.* Aldershot, UK: Ashgate 2008.

Efthymiadis, Stephanos. *Hagiography in Byzantium: Literature, Social History and Cult.* Variorum Collected Studies Series. London: Routledge, 2011.

"Episode 7: Hymns of Kassianí by Cappella Romana with Dr. Thomas Arentzen and Prof. Alexander Lingas." Dumbarton Oaks (Website). April 2021. https://www.doaks.org/research/byzantine/podcast/episode-7-hymns-by-kassiani.

Evangelical Lutheran Worship. Minneapolis: Evangelical Lutheran Church in America, 2006.

Fassler, Margot. "The First Marian Feast in Constantinople and Jerusalem: Chant Texts, Readings, and Homiletic Literature." In *The Study of Medieval Chant: Paths and Bridges, East and West,* edited by Peter Jefferey, 25–87. Woodbridge, Suffolk; Rochester, NY: Boydell, 2001.

Ferguson, Everett. *Baptism in the Early Church: History, Theology, and Liturgy in the First Five Centuries.* Grand Rapids: Eerdmans, 2009.

The Festal Menaion. Translated by Mother Mary. South Canaan, PA: St. Tikhon's Seminary Press, 1990.

Forostij, Teodor. "Від Різдва до Йордан." *Народна творчість та етнографія* nos. 1–2 (2001) 55–60.

Fotopoulos, John. "Some Common Misperceptions about the Date of Pascha/Easter." *Public Orthodoxy.* https://publicorthodoxy.org/2017/04/02/misperceptions-date-of-pascha/#more-2594.

Galadza, Daniel. *Liturgy and Byzantinization in Jerusalem.* Oxford Early Christian Studies. Oxford: Oxford University Press, 2018.

Getcha, Job. "Le Grand Canon pénitentiel de saint André de Crète. Une lecture typologique de l'histoire du salut." In *La liturgie, interprète de l'Écriture. II Dans les compositions liturgiques, prières et chants. Conférences Saint-Serge XLIXe Semaine d'Études Liturgiques 2002,* edited by Carlo Braga and Alessandro Pistoia, 105–20. Rome: Edizioni Liturgiche, 2003.

———. *The Typikon Decoded: An Explanation of Byzantine Liturgical Practice.* Orthodox Liturgy Series. Translated by P. Meyendorff. Yonkers, NY: St. Vladimir's Seminary Press, 2012.

The Great Octoechos. Nashua, NH: Sophia, 1999.

Griffin, Sean. *The Liturgical Past in Byzantium and Early Rus.* Cambridge: Cambridge University Press, 2019.

Grishin, Alexander. "Eastern Orthodox Iconography and Architecture." In *The Blackwell Companion to Eastern Christianity,* edited by Ken Parry, 371–87. Malden, MA: Blackwell, 2007.

Groen, Bert. "Anti-Judaism in the Present-Day Byzantine Liturgy." *Journal of Eastern Christian Studies* 60, nos. 1–4 (2008) 369–87.

———. "The Festival of the Presentation of the Lord: Its Origin, Structure and Theology in the Byzantine and Roman Rites. In *Christian Feast and Festival: The Dynamics of Western Liturgy and Culture*, edited by Paul Post, Gerard Rouwhorst, Louis van Tongeren, and Anton Scheer, 345–81. Leuvan, Belgium: Peters, 2001.

Hadžibulič, Sabina. "The *Slava* Celebration: A Private and a Public Matter." *Temenos: Nordic Journal of Comparative Religion* 53, no. 1 (2017) 31–53. https://doi.org/10.33356/temenos.51325.

Hannick, Christian. "The Theotokos in Byzantine Hymnography: Typology and Allegory." In *Images of the Mother of God*, edited by Maria Vassilaki, 69–78. London and New York: Routledge, 2005.

Hasluck, Margaret M. "The Basil-Cake of the Greek New Year." *Folklore* 38, no. 2 (June 30, 1927) 143–77. https://www.jstor.org/stable/1256522.

Hopko, Thomas. *The Lenten Spring: Readings for Great Lent*. Yonkers, NY: St. Vladimir's Seminary Press, 1998.

———. "St. Mary of Egypt." Ancient Faith Radio Podcasts, April 2, 2014. https://stpeterorthodoxchurch.com/fr-thomas-hopko-the-fifth-week-of-great-lent/.

———. *The Winter Pascha*. Yonkers, NY: St. Vladimir's Seminary Press, 1984.

Hovorun, Cyril. *Political Orthodoxies: The Unorthodoxies of the Church Coerced*. Minneapolis: Fortress, 2018.

Irwin, Kevin W. *Context and Text: A Method for Liturgical Theology*. Rev. ed. Collegeville, MN: Liturgical, 2018.

Jacob of Sarug. *Jacob of Sarug's Homilies on the Six Days of Creation*. Texts from Christian Late Antiquity. Edited and translated by Edward Mathews Jr. Piscataway, NJ: Gorgias, 2020.

Janeras, Sebastià. *La Vendredi-Saint dans la tradition liturgique byzantine*. Rome: Pontificio Anteno S. Anselmo, 1988.

Jeffreys, Elizabeth M., and Robert S. Nelson. "Akathistos Hymn." In *The Oxford Dictionary of Byzantium*, edited by Alexander P. Kazhdan. Oxford, UK: Oxford University Press, 1991. https://www.oxfordreference.com/view/10.1093/acref/9780195046526.001.0001/acref-9780195046526-e-0122.

John Paul II (Pope). "Dies Domini of the Holy Father John Paul II to the Bishops, Clergy and Faithful of the Catholic Church on Keeping the Lord's Day Holy." The Holy See (website). Written May 31, 1998. https://www.vatican.va/content/john-paul-ii/en/apost_letters/1998/documents/hf_jp-ii_apl_05071998_dies-domini.html.

Johnson, Maxwell. *The Rites of Christian Initiation*. Rev. ed. Collegeville, MN: Liturgical, 2007.

Kavanagh, Aidan. *Elements of Rite: A Handbook of Liturgical Style*. Collegeville, MN: Liturgical, 1990.

Krawchuk, Andrii, and Thomas Bremer. *Eastern Orthodox Encounters of Identity and Otherness: Values, Self-Reflection, Dialogues*. New York: Palgrave Macmillan, 2014.

Krueger, Derek. *Liturgical Subjects: Christian Ritual, Biblical Narrative, and the Formation of the Self in Byzantium*. Philadelphia: University of Pennsylvania Press, 2014.

Lambertsen, Isaac E. *Saint Job of Pochaev: Life, Liturgical Service, and Akathist Hymn*. Liberty, TN: St. John of Kronstadt, 1997.

Larin, Vassa. "Feasting and Fasting According to the Byzantine Typikon." *Worship* 83, no. 2 (2009) 133–48.

Larson-Miller, Lizette. "Consuming Time." *Worship* 88, no. 6 (2014) 528–43.

The Lenten Triodion. Translated by Mother Mary and Archimandrite Kallistos Ware. South Canaan, PA: St. Tikhon's Seminary Press, 2002.

Lukashevich, A. "всех святых, в земле российской просиявщих, неделя." *Pravoslavnaia entsyklopedia* (website). May 28, 2009. https://www.pravenc.ru/text/155558.html.

Maraval, Pierre, Manuel C. Díaz y Díaz, and Szent Bierzo-I Valerius. *Égérie, journal de voyage*. Paris: Cerf, 1982.

Mateos, Juan. *La celebration de la parole dans la liturgie byzantine*. Orientalia christiana analecta 191. Rome: Edizioni Orientalia Christiana, 1971.

———. "Le cycle des fetes mobiles." In *Le Typicon de la Grande Église*, 165.

———. *Le Typicon de la Grande Église*. Orientalia christiana analecta. Rome: Pont. Institutum Orientalium Studiorum, 1962.

Maylor, Elizabeth A. "Serial Position Effects in Semantic Memory: Reconstructing the Order of Verses of Hymns." *Psychonomic Bulletin & Review* 9, no. 4 (December 2002) 816–20. https://doi.org/10.3758/bf03196340.

McDonnell, Kilian. *The Baptism of Jesus in the Jordan: The Trinitarian and Cosmic Order of Salvation*. Collegeville, MN: Liturgical, 1996.

McGuckin, John Anthony. *The Eastern Orthodox Church: A New History*. New Haven: Yale University Press, 2020.

Meyendorff, Paul. *The Anointing of the Sick*. Orthodox Liturgy Series. Yonkers, NY: St. Vladimir's Seminary Press, 2009.

A Monk of the Eastern Church (Lev Gillet). *The Year of Grace of the Lord: A Scriptural and Liturgical Commentary on the Calendar of the Orthodox Church*. Yonkers, NY: St. Vladimir's Seminary Press, 1980.

Monks of New Skete. *Passion and Resurrection*. Cambridge, NY: New Skete, 1995.

Morozowich, Mark M. *Holy Thursday in the Jerusalem and Constantinopolitan Traditions: The Liturgical Celebrations from the Fourth to the Fourteenth Centuries*. Rome: Pontificium Institutum, 2002.

Mureşan, Dan Ioan. "The Romanian Tradition." In *The Orthodox Christian World*, edited by Augustine Casiday, 140–52. London and New York: Routledge, 2012.

Orthodox Church in America. "Nativity of the Holy Glorious Prophet, Forerunner and Baptist, John—Troparion & Kontakion: Troparion—Tone 4." Orthodox Church in America (website). Updated June 24, 2022. https://www.oca.org/saints/lives/2000/06/24/101800-nativity-of-the-holy-glorious-prophet-forerunner-and-baptist-joh.

———. "Saint John Chysostom, Archbishop of Constantinople: The Paschal Sermon." Orthodox Church in America (website). Updated 2022. https://www.oca.org/fs/sermons/the-paschal-sermon.

Ouspensky, Leonid, and Vladimir Lossky. *The Meaning of Icons*. 2nd ed. Yonkers, NY: St. Vladimir's Seminary Press, 1999.

Overstreet, Michael F., and Alice F. Healy. "Item and Order Information in Semantic Memory: Students' Retention of the 'CU Fight Song' Lyrics." *Memory & Cognition* 39 (2011) 251–59. doi.org/10.3758/s13421-010-0018-3.

Pargament, Kenneth I., and Donald V. DeRosa. "What Was that Sermon About? Predicting Memory for Religious Messages from Cognitive Psychological Theory." *Journal for the Scientific Study of Religion* 24, no. 2 (June 1985) 180–93. https://doi.org/10.2307/1386341.

Patterson Ševčenko, Nancy. "Virgin Hodegetria." In *The Oxford Dictionary of Byzantium*, edited by Alexander Kazhdan. Oxford, UK: Oxford University Press, 1991.

Pentcheva, Bissera. *Icons and Power: The Mother of God in Byzantium.* State College, PA: Penn State University Press, 2006.

The Pentecostarion. Rev. 2nd ed. Boston: Holy Transfiguration Monastery, 2014.

Plekon, Michael. *Hidden Holiness.* Notre Dame: University of Notre Dame Press, 2009.

Plokhy, Serhii. *The Gates of Europe: A History of Ukraine.* New York: Basic Books, 2017.

———. *Unmaking Imperial Russia: Mykhailo Hrushevsky and the Writing of Ukrainian History.* Toronto: University of Toronto Press, 2014.

Podskalsky, Gerhard, Robert Taft, and Annemarie Weyl Carr. "Transfiguration." In *The Oxford Dictionary of Byzantium,* edited by Alexander Kazdhan. Oxford: Oxford University Press, 1995. https://www.oxfordreference.com/view/10.1093/acref/9780195046526.001.0001/acref-9780195046526-e-5561.

Pott, Thomas. *Byzantine Liturgical Reform: A Study of Liturgical Change in the Byzantine Tradition.* Orthodox Liturgy Series. Yonkers, NY: St. Vladimir's Seminary Press, 2010.

Renoux, Athanase. *Le codex arménien Jérusalem 121.* Brepols, Belgium: Brepols Publishers, 1969.

Riabkov, Vladimir M. "Maslenitsa in the Historiography of Socio-Cultural Activities." *Ethnic Culture* 2, no. 3 (2020) 42–51. https://doi.org/10.31483/r-74919.

Roll, Susan. *Towards the Origins of Christmas.* Kampen, Netherlands: Kok Pharos, 1995.

Roman Missal, English translation according to the third typical edition. Study edition. Collegeville, MN: Liturgical, 2010.

Rordorf, Willy. *Sunday: The History of the Day of Rest and Worship in the Earliest Centuries of the Christian Church.* London: SCM, 1968.

Russo, Nicholas V. "The Origins of Lent." PhD diss., University of Notre Dame, 2010. ProQuest AAT 3441749.

Schmemann, Alexander. *Great Lent: Journey to Pascha.* Yonkers, NY: St. Vladimir's Seminary Press, 1969.

Schulz, Hans Joachim. *Byzantine Liturgy: Symbolic Structure and Faith Expression.* Collegeville, MN: Liturgical, 1992.

Searle, Mark. "Sunday: The Heart of the Liturgical Year." In *Between Memory and Hope: Readings on the Liturgical Year,* edited by Maxwell E. Johnson, 59–76. Collegeville, MN: Liturgical, 2000.

Service and Akathist: To Our Father Among the Saints John Archbishop of Shanghai and San Francisco the Wonderworker. San Francisco: Russkiy Pastyr, originally published in 2004; 2013 revision.

Shevzov, Vera. "Miracle-working Icons, Laity, and Authority in the Russian Orthodox Church, 1861–1917." *The Russian Review* 58, no. 1 (January 1999) 26–48.

———. "Petitions to the Holy Synod Regarding Miraculous Icons." In *Orthodox Christianity in Imperial Russia: A Source Book on Lived Religion,* edited by Heather Coleman, 229–48. Bloomington: Indiana University Press, 2014.

———. "Women on the Fault Lines of Faith: Pussy Riot and the Insider/Outsider Challenge to Post-Soviet Orthodoxy." *Religion and Gender* 4, no. 2 (December 2014) 121–45.

"Slujba Sfantului Andrei Saguna." Crestin Ortodox (Website). January 27, 2022. https://www.crestinortodox.ro/slujbe-randuieli/slujba-sfantului-andrei-saguna-141758.html.

Stewart-Sykes, Alistair. *On Pascha: Melito of Sardis.* Popular Patristics Series. Yonkers, NY: St. Vladimir's Seminary Press, 2001.

Streza, Dan A. "The Orthodox Liturgical Year and Its Theological Structure." *HTS Theological Studies* 77, no. 4 (2021) 1–8. https://doi.org/10.4102/hts.v77i4.6742.

Subtelny, Orest. *Ukraine: A History.* 4th ed. Toronto: University of Toronto Press, 2009.

Taft, Robert. *Beyond East and West: Problems in Liturgical Understanding.* Rome: Edizioni Orientalia Christiana Pontifical Oriental, 2001.

———. *A History of the Liturgy of St. John.* Chicago: Loyola, 1978.

———. "Holy Week in the Byzantine Tradition." In *Hebdomadae Sanctae Celebratio: Conspectus Historicus Comparativus: The Celebration of Holy Week in Ancient Jerusalem and Its Development in the Rites of East and West,* edited by A. G. Kolamparampil, 67–91. Rome: CLV—Edizioni liturgiche, 1997.

———. "In the Bridegroom's Absence. The Paschal Triduum in the Byzantine Church." In *Liturgy in Byzantium and Beyond,* 71–97. New York: Routledge, 1995.

———. *Liturgy in Byzantium and Beyond.* New York: Routledge, 1995.

Taft, Robert, and Annemarie Weyl Carr. "Annunciation." In *The Oxford Dictionary of Byzantium,* edited by Alexander P. Kazhdan. Oxford, UK: Oxford University Press, 1991. https://www.oxfordreference.com/view/10.1093/acref/9780195046526.001.0001/acref-9780195046526-e-0300.

Talley, Thomas. *The Origins of the Liturgical Year.* 2nd ed. Collegeville, MN: Liturgical, 1986.

Tanner, Norman. *Decrees of the Ecumenical Councils.* 2 vols. Washington, DC: Georgetown University Press, 2017.

Tarchnisvili, Michel. *Le Grand Lectionnaire de L'Eglise de Jerusalem.* Nos. 1126–33. Corpus Scriptorium Christianorum Orientalium. Leuven, Belgium: Peeters, 1959.

The Times. "The Times View on the Russian Patriarch's Backing for the War in Ukraine: Church and State." March 21, 2022. https://www.thetimes.co.uk/article/the-times-view-on-the-russian-patriarchs-backing-for-the-war-in-ukraine-church-and-state-36lq3f9z9.

Tkachenko, Alexander. "Год Церковный." *Православная Энциклопедия* (Website). April 7, 2011. https://www.pravenc.ru/text/165235.html

Typikon. *Тѵпїконъ сіесть уставъ.* Moscow: Publishing Council of the Russian Orthodox Church, 2002.

von Gardner, Johann. *Russian Church Singing: Orthodox Worship and Hymnography.* Yonkers, NY: St. Vladimir's Seminary Press, 1980.

Wainwright, Geoffrey. "Sacramental Time." *Studia Liturgica* 14, nos. 2–4 (December 1982) 135–47. https://doi.org/10.1177/0039320782014002-411.

Ware, Timothy. *The Orthodox Church: An Introduction to Eastern Christianity.* 3rd rev. ed. New York: Penguin, 2015.

Wellesz, Egon. *The Akathistos Hymn: Introduced and Transcribed by E. Wellesz.* Copenhagen: Munksgaard, 1957.

World Council of Churches. "Towards a Common Date for Easter." World Council of Churches. March 10, 1997. https://www.oikoumene.org/resources/documents/towards-a-common-date-for-easter.

Wortley, John. "The Marian Relics at Constantinople." *Greek, Roman and Byzantine Studies* 45 (2005): 171–87.

Zugravu, Gheorghita. "Kassia the Melodist. And the Making of a Byzantine Hymnographer." PhD diss, Columbia University, 2013.

Printed in Great Britain
by Amazon

26437357R00101